BEING BERNADETTE:

From Polite Silence to Finding the Black Girl Magic Within

Dedicated to the four amazing women who helped to groom and shape me into the woman I am today. Had it not been for the grace of God, mentorship, and a praying grandmother, my story would have been different. My auntie Blandina, the anchor of the family; my mother, the most courageous woman on earth; my life mentor and coach, Patricia Murphy; and most importantly, my grandmother, Lizzie Green.

My grandmother demonstrated unconditional love each day. She was a prayer warrior, full of humor, and the first black feminist I knew. She was a force to be reckoned with and protected us like a hawk. I continue to repeat the Psalms chapters she taught me (27, 86, 91, 100—just to name a few) when I'm in distress, need a heavenly hug from her, or just crying because I'm filled with pure joy. Her favorite three words were "Jesus, help me." These words have become my own.

Contents

Foreword

The journey of Being is one of the most challenging and exhilarating experiences in life. It is an indicator that two occurrences have happened: a person has experienced darkness and elected to embrace light. That is what Carol Tonge Mack has done as she has written her memoir, *Being Bernadette*. Carol taps into those deep dark places that we usually try to keep hidden in order to share her journey for moving to her next level of excellence. In the process, she stepped into understanding that her light and life matter and must be magnified. *Being Bernadette* highlights, in a very comfortable and enjoyable way, what it means to face life's challenges and keep moving forward to bring dreams and goals to life. Carol's vivid description of her homeland in Antigua, contrasted with the view of what life in the United States provided, helps to set the stage for bringing you into her world. Her direct method of communicating—both in person and with her writing style—helps to cut to the chase of key takeaways that can be applied to your life.

Dark periods don't define you. We will all have challenges in this life. As I share with my Dreamwalking® Family, once you obtain clarity and determine that you will bring your dreams to life with a sense of urgency, the fiery darts, designed to get you off task and unfocused, will show up consistently and with great fierceness. You will need strategies and a level of intentionality to stay on track and do what God purposed for your life as he formed you in your mother's womb. Carol has shown that no matter what comes your way, you can leverage it and move forward with urgency and a 'by any means necessary' attitude. It's important to note that surrounding yourself with like-minded people and having a mentor to remind you that your past does not indicate your future are critical to achieving big dreams that deliver big results.

Reach for the light. One of the things that I had to do, as I was experiencing darkness, was to use every ounce of my being to reach for the light. I knew if I could figure out how to get there, I would be able to move to my next level of excellence. It's hard work. It's lonely. It's exasperating. It's exhilarating. It's empowering. It's an evolution...it's a revolution of your spirit. Walking in the light gives you a sense of being that completes the journey of Being in a very special way. Walking in the light unleashes power that, quite frankly, is hard to contain once you learn how to effectively manage it.

Let your passion move you past your pain in order to find your voice. Use Carol's strategies to inspire you to ignite your fire and bring forth your greatness so that you are silent no more. Use your voice and magnify your light. Get on the journey of Being! The world is waiting!

—Sonia Jackson Myles, Founder & CEO of The Sister Accord LLC and Chief Dreamwalker

Acknowledgments

I am extremely grateful to those precious people in my life who helped to ensure the completion of this book. Over twenty years ago, my mother told me I should write a book. However, it wasn't my time then, but she planted the seed. Thank you Robin Martin and Sonia Jackson Myles for the final nudge to make this memoir a reality. To my dearest friends who listened, comforted, and hugged me when I needed it the most, I can't thank you enough. Marilyn Kershaw, Tyree Gaines, Yolanda Cooper, Lori Wright, and Cecily Goode, I don't know what I would've done without your support on those days when I was at my lowest.

Thank you, Doug Cooper Spencer, Phyllis Jeffers-Coly, and William Jackson for the critical feedback and the constructive conversations even when you didn't have time. Special thanks to the editor, Jerome Clark, who can turn raw, emotional words into a story that matters. The creative genius behind the design of the book cover, Greg Cooper Spencer, your gift is undeniable. Steven Edinburg and Crystal Edinburg, thank you both for enhancing my beauty with the awesome photoshoot. Harry Richards and Judy Spiller, thank you for the opportunity to sit in, listen, and learn during crucial administrative meetings; it was my first exposure to workplace politics. The experience had an indelible effect on my expectations of other supervisors.

Ron Jackson, thanks for acknowledging my professional skills and providing a "real" seat with a voice at the table. We were both dealt a different set of cards, but as they say in church, joy cometh in the morning.

To the students who made my job easy, it was my honor to serve you. I will continue to advocate for you by any means necessary. I can't forget to thank Renee, Pam, and Claire who always demonstrated kindness and treated me like family.

To my boisterous NYC family and my brother Tony Mwingira, for always having my back and reminding me that I can always come home, thank you from the bottom of my heart. Lots of love to the Mack and West families for supporting my success in any form. My prayer warriors and my Black Women on the Move sisters, you are exceptional, and I am proud that you opened your heart and welcomed me. My two amazing children who keep me grounded, you are truly the best part of me. I am eternally indebted to my husband, James, for making me believe that love and partnership really conquer all.

Introduction

We all have a story. I honestly didn't think my story was worth telling. Why would it be any different from the countless personal narratives in the world? My friend Robin convinced me that my story matters; it was my life and my truth.

I am, unapologetically, a black woman. I have feelings—feelings of love and anguish. I love my family passionately. Life can be messy because we're human. But if only one person outside of my family reads my story, then at least my voice has been heard.

There's nothing like the feeling of being powerless, speechless, not having a voice, being silenced, and never being invited to the table. I prefer that I not be invited to the table if I'm not served the same food as everyone else. Other people are comfortable just being in the room. Not me. Sometimes we accept leftovers, like slaves who were given the scraps from the master's table. Will we continue to settle for the scraps?

A couple of things that I learned in college are you must speak with honesty and vigor and must know thyself first. Yet being authentic isn't always accepted, especially at work. It often depends on who you are. For me and others like me, if we dislike or disagree with anything, or if we show our displeasure, we're angry black women. Moreover, implicit in it all, we don't even have a right to be.

So it's time to write my own narrative. It may not change the world, but I want my voice to be heard. My story may resonate strongly with some people or not at all. But I hope it resonates with people whatever their stature in life; maybe where they feel silenced.

I also hope my story reaches the young girl who thinks her pregnancy will stop her dreams. I want her to see that it's just a setback or a setup for a comeback. To the black woman sitting in a cubicle thinking, "Is this ever going to be over?" Yes, it will. You just have to write, steal, take, or snatch your own freedom papers. Harriet Tubman isn't coming for you. And don't wait too long to "get on the bus" or any other mode of transportation. You simply have to believe and act.

To the immigrant hoping to find the American dream, the cultural barriers are real, especially your accent and the way you may pronounce certain words. Some Americans can be unforgiving, but you can thrive and succeed.

I hope this resonates with the girl in the economically disadvantaged neighborhood sitting in class thinking: How am I going to accomplish my dreams? How am I going to get out of this apartment and own my house? Will a college education actually help me? What else will work? I don't see a way out.

To the single, young girl who has diapers and clothes to buy but must depend on the kindness of strangers or family members to make ends meet, keep your head up! Find the right mentor who is going to pour into your spirit. You may not always like the advice, but at least there's someone who will listen and give feedback. You must have people around who care about you enough to tell you when you're wrong. Know that it is going to get better. It has to, because to have some type of sanity, there is no other way but up.

Chapter One

A Caribbean Girl Takes on the Streets of New York City

As a young teen, I came to this country with my sister Lisa and the assumption that life would be easier. I knew life would be different because of our transition from one country to another. New York City wasn't the Caribbean. The South Bronx—specifically Soundview—was not Greenbay or Gray's Farm. I had seen snowfall, but that was on television. I had heard stories of people trekking through snow, sleet, and freezing temperatures to get to school and to work, but that all seemed like fun to me. The snowball fights. Sticking your tongue out trying to catch the snowflakes. Drinking hot chocolate and apple cider. To me, those were all fun things.

I brought with me most of the clothes and shoes I had accumulated over the years. On TV, I saw children with special toys, like a stuffed animal, doll, or blanket, which made them feel safe. I didn't have any such toy, but I treasured my grandmother's head wrap. I loved the smell of her hair. She used coconut oil as a moisturizer for her hair. I didn't want to ever wash the wrap because I had no idea when I would see her again. I wanted to preserve her presence, and the wrap allowed me to feel her near me. My grandmother exuded love from every pore of her body. I really believed that if I kept the wrap and occasionally smelled her scent of love, I would feel her close to me. And I did.

I also brought a cultural skirt that I had worn earlier, during my school's queen competition. It reminded me of the childhood I felt I was giving up. I didn't know where my other relatives in New York were, and I didn't know if I would be able to see them. The happiness I had in Antigua was gone, and I couldn't imagine what might lie ahead.

America, where people walked on streets of gold. I bought into that dream for a while when I encountered the city's bright lights. I remember our plane landing like it was yesterday. There were so many lights; it was absolutely amazing. As we drove through the streets and highways, I was mesmerized by the tall buildings; the taxis; the long, wide freeways; and just so many people. I was so excited. America—this must be what heaven feels like or so I thought. But nothing was further from the truth.

When we finally got out of the car, we went not to a house but to an apartment. I didn't understand. Back in Antigua, we had a four-bedroom house, with a yard, coconut trees, guavas, and mango trees all within a few steps. And now we were in an apartment? Why? Were we not in America, where life was better? We stayed in a basement apartment with limited space; boxes were packed against the wall because they were preparing to move with the addition to the family, my sister Sharon. I got very little sleep that night. Still, I couldn't wait to see New York City in the daylight. I wanted to know what the people were like and what the streets were like. I wanted to know if I would see any resemblance of home. Maybe this was going to be so great that I wouldn't miss Antigua.

So we moved into a two-bedroom apartment unit on the third floor of a building between 170th Street and Whyte Place near the Grand Concourse. It was bigger than the basement, but it required three different keys to get all the way inside of it: one key for the outside door and two other keys for the front door. How was this possible, just to get into your own home? But the apartment was always clean. My mother would have it no other way. Pine Sol and Clorox were our friends. She worked all day and some holidays cleaning the homes of other people, and there was no way she would come home to a dirty place. After Lisa and I completed our household chores, my mother would swipe her finger over the table, sink, or dresser, and it had better be clean or we wouldn't hear the end of it.

The windows in our living room gave me the best view of the block we lived on. I had never seen so many people in one place. They looked like they were going somewhere. Why were they in such a hurry? They didn't look relaxed. I rarely heard greetings like my grandmother used to give our neighbors. The people here spoke different languages and had so many different skin tones. The elderly people didn't get the respect I was used to seeing them get, which I thought was odd. Pets seemed like family members— licking the faces of their owners in public—instead of like animals that belonged in the yard or under the house, and certainly not living inside the apartment. The people and their pets were all strangers to me. I wondered if I would survive outside of our apartment.

At first, Lisa and I were allowed to go only to the supermarket while my mother was away. She literally gave us a trial run by walking us downstairs, then to the supermarket, buying items, giving the money to the cashier, walking back home without interacting with anyone, and finally opening the apartment door with the keys. We were told to never—and I mean never—open the door to anyone, not even the police. She said, "They're going to have to break down the door if they need anything. You can't trust anyone. Just because they're wearing uniforms doesn't mean they're police officers." Maybe that's one of the reasons I have trust issues, especially with the law.

When I woke up on most mornings, I rushed to the window and peeked outside. I was disappointed. The streets were not filled with gold. Outside, it was warm, but I didn't feel the island breeze. I didn't smell the fresh grass. I didn't hear the crowing of the roosters or my grandmother's pleasant voice greeting everyone who walked by the window with her neighborly "good morning!" I don't know why I thought the streets would be spotless. Growing up, I had heard stories about what America looked like, and I had seen many TV shows. Family members who visited the island or friends who lived in the U.S. never had a genuine conversation about life in NYC. Since I'm a people watcher, I made some assumptions based on how they were dressed. They had what looked like expensive clothes, shoes, lots of jewelry, hair always perfect—and their kids dressed accordingly. Little did I know, that was part of the brainwashing; they, too, were brainwashed to show others a life that may not be real. I soon found that there was nothing like living the experience yourself.

Today, I would tell anyone coming to America hoping to achieve his or her dreams that the streets are not paved with gold. The streets are tough. One must learn to defend oneself, and sometimes that means defending oneself physically. I remember the block fights, and how it's easy to get caught in the middle of one. I remember hearing gunshots, and those were common. I remember loud music, laughter, and arguments. And although craziness happens everywhere, violence has a way of finding the schoolyard across the street. I saw the yellow police tape at the crime scene. I imagined the dead bodies a few feet away from the school steps where just hours earlier we had played. I didn't know the victims personally, but I thought about them for months afterwards. Yes, you hear these kinds of stories, but you never imagine it would happen right on the next block that you can see from your window.

Rumors of police interrogations and the large holes left by the penetration of bullets in the back of the building are seared in my memory. It all changed my life forever. I rarely talk about it now; it's too hard for me to grapple with what happened. Even getting to school was a struggle. Crack cocaine was a hot commodity. I saw the drug addicts, crack pipes, the vials, and other drug paraphernalia on the streets on my way to school. There were abandoned buildings, and sometimes I didn't know if someone would come out of the buildings and harm me. But I stayed focused. I walked swiftly and told myself I just had to get through three blocks from the train station to get to school. As long as I was in the school building, I felt safe.

I was Antiguan, and until I came to this country, I rarely had to identify myself or my closest friends as being black, or any color. Where I came from, light skin versus dark skin was never an issue among my friends and family. Here it was an issue. Several fights in school involved a dark-skinned person against a light-skinned person. I thought it was interesting that, for instance, a dark-skinned young girl would make sure to cut or scratch the face of a light-skinned girl as a way to mar what she perceived as her beauty.

I discovered that, as an immigrant black person, native blacks would treat me like crap because they thought I was trying to take something from them. Job-taking was the subject of many discussions. Children often repeated what they heard at home. "They're taking the cleaning jobs. They're taking the jobs at the supermarket. They're taking the jobs in the stockroom. They're taking the jobs in the hotels." And there was more taking of jobs than there were jobs. Other children whispered about the non-brand-name clothing I wore, which I didn't understand. I was unfamiliar with the importance of wearing certain types of clothing. We were from a country where wearing uniforms to school every day was the norm. The information in your head was more important for your future. Even other immigrant children who arrived years earlier teased me about my accent, even though they didn't speak much better than I did. I figured that was their way of showing or telling me they'd been here first, as if they were marking their territory.

They also isolated immigrants. I felt like there were four types of people on the playground: the black Americans (quasi-native, if you will); immigrants who had been here many years; the newly arrived immigrants (I was part of that crew); and children of immigrants. One would think all the immigrants would stick together or at least speak up for each other, but this was the playground, and pure Darwinism at its best. It was survival of the most perceived integrated.

I started to wonder if I had the right complexion. I was told I was dark-skinned, a term I had never before used to describe myself. For when you grow up with a black prime minister, a black governor, a black police force, black news anchors, doctors, entrepreneurs, bus drivers, and so on, the color of someone's skin is the furthest thing from your mind. Dark-skinned versus light-skinned was a foreign concept to me. My grandmother had taught me to treat all people the same, that we were all children of God. I couldn't imagine demeaning someone because of her or his skin tone. I had my first fight with a girl who wanted to show her friends her bravado and that she could fight; I know she thought, "she had it like that." But I wasn't hearing any of it. She was a mixture of black and Puerto Rican. We were going to fight after school, and she had two or three other girls with her to make sure no one else jumped in. I don't know who won the fight, but my mother told me to never come home without getting a few punches in and possibly drawing blood. And that's what I did. I learned quickly what to do when there's a fight. I had my Vaseline ready, my hairpins, and my scrunchies, but I forgot to take my earrings off. What was I thinking? I still have the extra slit on my left ear, but I never forgot after that day. And to this day, Vaseline serves many purposes, but I always have a small jar in my bag just in case.

I had to constantly prove myself, and I sensed a lot of jealousy because I kept showing them that I was better than what they were saying about me. My feelings were: Yes, I am not American, and yes, I have an accent, but I'm just as good as you are. I won trophies and awards in middle school. The road was not easy, and it was not clear. The road was definitely not paved with gold. In fact, the road was a struggle. But I know now why that struggle was so important. It prepared me mentally for the challenges I would face later on.

Chapter Two

The Boogie Down Posse

I attended Samuel Gompers Vocational Technical High School in New York City. In junior high, we had all been given a thick booklet to consider our academic and career options. I knew for sure then that I didn't want to go to the high school that was closest to where I lived. I would have been home in less than ten minutes. What high school student wants to live that close to the school? Furthermore, I had heard about the fights at that school, and I saw the police cars in front of the school almost daily. There were rumors about illicit activities in the hallways and staircases, and I didn't want to be a part of it. I didn't want my mother having to leave her hourly job as a maid to take me home because of a fight.

I had cousins who lived nearby. One of my cousins, Dee as we called him, was the kind of guy who would beat your ass first then ask questions later. He was extremely protective of his sisters and his cousins. He carried a baseball bat in his luxury car—as a skilled auto mechanic, he could be found driving a Pathfinder, a Lexus, or a Maxima, as he was very skilled in auto mechanics. But I didn't want his watchful eyes on me at every turn, so when I visited Gompers, which was a few stops on the No. 6 train, I decided I would go there.

Back then we had tube TVs and radios that students could disassemble and calculate the resistance, current, and voltage. I was fascinated with capacitors and being able to know what was wrong with the TV at home and not have to bang it on the sides to see the picture clearly. When I first visited Gompers, the teachers showed us what the students there were learning, and they described the types of jobs that awaited students after graduation. Some would get jobs at the local telephone or cable company. At the time, the salary seemed like a lot of money. The thought of an eighteen-year-old, with little or no money, making thousands of dollars—more money than her parents made in a year—was so enticing. However, going to college was always part of my plan. "By hook or by crook," I was going to get there. Those were my mother's words.

I vaguely remember the first day of high school. I recall being nervous because I started in the tenth grade.

Most of the students in my grade had already known each other for at least a year. To make matters worse, it was a new neighborhood. I started to have doubts about my decision to go to Gompers, but there was no turning back now. I had my book bag, new clothes, new shoes, and seven new one-subject notebooks, all in different colors. They all had to fit in my Trapper Keeper. My stop on the No. 6 train was at Longfellow Avenue. I didn't like this station. The stop was underground—very different from Soundview. The natural light makes a difference when you're a young girl traveling alone. When underground, the area near the back of the last car is not well-lit, and the stench when the wind from the passing train hits your nose is repugnant. Some days there was a homeless man on the bench at the station. He always spoke to himself loudly, had several bags, and wore tattered clothing; he may have had mental problems. There was no eye contact, my mother told us to mind our business and keep moving. I also had to figure out which exit wouldn't place me on the same side with all the auto mechanic body shops. The gawking mechanics, at least twice my age and older, would yell out to me, "Hey, mama!" Or they would whistle at me. If I got too close, they would reach for my hand or tug at my shirt.

Back then, I didn't know anything about harassment. I viewed it as men perhaps interested in inappropriate conversations, which could lead to other mischief. But I learned my lesson after the first few encounters, and I started using the other exit. At first the whistles made me feel special, when three or four men are suddenly interested in you or your body. But my mother taught me that some men only wanted one thing—SEX. So, I took the compliments, kept moving, and I never stopped to hear if they had anything more to say. You can imagine the challenges. It was a battleground.

Samuel Gompers High School was a much larger building than junior high school. The doors were wide, long, and heavy. They were made of brass or some type of metal, almost like an old church. As I approached the steps, my heart skipped a beat as I was greeted by a security officer and metal detectors. They were supposed to keep us safe. But like anything else, teenagers find ways around any rule.

The staircase on the left of the entrance led upstairs to the main office and to the principal's office, one place you may or may not want to be. Ms. Hawthorne, the principal, was a woman who meant business. One could be in her office either for excelling in class or for bad behavior. She had high expectations of all her students and her teachers too. And she actually reached out to the custodial staff and made them feel like they were a part of the overall effort to help the students. When we disobeyed the rules or didn't follow the school code, she didn't make us feel like bad teenagers, but like students who made poor decisions. She always looked polished, professional, and classy. She wore nice jewelry, and not even one hair was out of place. I thought that her whole attire must have been expensive. And I asked myself, "Who dresses the way she does and regularly talks to the janitors?" I hoped and I wanted, so much, for the people at my mother's job to treat her the same way.

Like any high school, the hallways at Gompers were bustling with students going to and from their lockers or the bathroom to gossip, to continue the trash-talking from the day before, to plan card games during lunch, to prepare for the next class, or to get a posse ready for a fight after school. I was more concerned about adjusting to the new environment and not getting into fights. I heard conversations about Boricuas or Puerto Ricans, Dominicans,

Haitians, or people from one of the other Latin American countries. There was discord between Dominicans and Haitians. There was discord between Dominicans and Puerto Ricans. I was just the girl they thought was from Jamaica, and most days I didn't correct them.

Clothing brands were also a hot topic. My mother didn't care what brand I wore. If it wasn't on sale, she wasn't buying it. She would repeat something my grandmother said to her, "Wah you have inna you head, betta than anyting else, no worry 'bout wah nobody say." I thought, that's easier said than done because she wasn't going to Gompers during these times. She didn't go to high school in the United States; she had no idea how brutal these kids could be. But I was one of the top three students in my grade, so most of the name-calling toward me was along the lines of "teacher's pet," or something else that was not too demeaning but hurt nonetheless. Besides, if you were mean to one of the smart girls, who was going to help you with your homework or with class projects? By being a good student, it was like having a built-in protective cover against verbal assaults.

Still, I rolled deep with at least six to eight people in high school, including Mario and the crew and about ten in the neighborhood. I never went to the movies with fewer than five people; we protected each other at all costs. No one was going to tell me, "Run those sneakers, Shorty!" No one was going to snatch the diamond-cut chain from my neck when my posse was around. We didn't threaten anyone, but everyone knew not to bother us when walking on the street or riding the train. But there was always one person in our group who made us shake our damn heads or regret that they came with us.

One of my favorite pastimes was going to the movies at Whitestone with the posse from the block, my sister, my cousins Juleen and Lucy, and meeting up with other friends. At one point, we had almost twenty people in the group. Unfortunately, others felt threatened by our presence. Some of them thought that we looked like roughnecks or thugs. I can't remember a time I wore a skirt or a dress, other than at weddings or special events at church. A dress was not my favorite attire, because you know, I had to always be ready to run. I had Timberland boots, baggy jeans, a T-shirt or sweatshirt, jewelry, a Kangol hat turned backwards, my gold Nefertiti tooth cap, and yes, sunglasses at night. Who really was going to say something to me, dressed like that? I used to think I was fresher than fresh and as fly as some of the hip-hop artists.

Looking back, I realize that my high school experiences had a huge impact on my personal development, my friendships, and how I interact with others. My high school and the neighborhood helped prepare me for my professional life. And the street corners taught me skills that higher education could not.

Before going to college, though, I had to think differently. In so doing, I let go of my urban posse, and I traded that for the lush, green mountains of Vermont. Once there, I met other students from the South Bronx, Brooklyn, and other cities in the northeast and around the country. The Caribbean posse was in full effect; it wasn't too difficult to find my niche. I chose a college that was six hours away from home because I knew I wouldn't be distracted by friends, by the city's bright lights, or traveling twice a day on the train. I needed and welcomed this new journey and the opportunity to learn in a different environment.

Honestly, it reminded me a little bit of Antigua as I drove through the small towns of New England. The cows and other farm animals were very familiar, especially the scent of fresh grass, something I rarely experienced in New York City, unless I went to Central Park. I loved looking out into the distance and seeing nothing, yet seeing everything. The sun touching the last mountain looked like a postcard in the dentist's office. Not like a place where people actually lived. As much as I was ready for this new adventure, I was apprehensive about going to a college that was predominantly white. From the Caribbean, to the streets of New York City, and now, to rural Vermont. What was I thinking?

I loved the college visit. I spent the night on campus. I met some students from the Bronx, and they promised to be there if I enrolled. It was completely different from other schools I visited.

I thought I'd become an engineer, since I loved math and excelled in it. But calculus didn't love me back when I first got a taste of it in a math course I took before going to college. I changed my mind about becoming an engineer, but I had no idea what major I'd pursue. I loved learning. But learning what? Of all the courses I had during my first year of college, sociology, African-American studies, and history came to the forefront. I loved history while I was in high school, and it certainly helped that my favorite teacher taught social studies. World War II facts, the Tiananmen Square protest, and local politics like finding the killer of the Central Park jogger, rolled off her tongue so easily. I thought, surely, I can do this as well. The more history classes I took, the more I fell in love with it. I decided that history was the best major for me.

Learning about my own culture, history, and heritage was in my blood and part of my DNA. But when I learned that history majors had to write a junior and senior thesis, I was crushed. Sure, in high school we had to write a few papers. But to me, none of that compared to the research, writing, rewriting, review, and more writing, which were expectations in college. I felt it was too much. However, years later, I am using those writing skills in my professional and personal life. At the time, I didn't realize how my liberal arts education would help me in my career, and how valuable it was.

Chapter Three

Say It Ain't So

I became sexually active when I was eighteen. I felt I was ready. I had heard a lot of talk from the boys at school about the girls with whom they had sex. Most of that talk wasn't pleasant. They called some of the girls whores, tramps, and easy to get in bed. I didn't want to be one of those girls. And sex outside of marriage was considered sinful and not godly. At least that's what I learned in church back in Antigua. That played a major role in my personal decision to wait before engaging in sex. My mother got pregnant with me when she was sixteen, but I didn't view her as being ungodly.

I made it through high school without a pregnancy and started using birth control pills when I went to college, and I thought I was being consistent. If I missed taking a pill one day, I'd take two pills the next day. I figured this double-up system would work. I had forgotten the crucial part of a conversation I had with a nurse. In that conversation, she told me to set an alarm and take the pill at the same time each day. I thought that if I doubled the dosage, then after missing a day, I should still be protected. What could really go wrong?

~ ~ ~

I started seeing him when I was in high school. He lived two buildings to the west, so I saw him most days. Like any young love, I wanted to see him every day, but that wasn't possible. If I didn't see him outside, I contacted him on his black beeper. We talked on the phone sometimes, but we only had one phone in the apartment, and it was in the kitchen. It was a rotary phone, tan-colored, with a long cord that was always twisted. We did not have call-waiting yet, so I could not talk for long. If my mother tried to call and the phone was busy, there was a lot of explaining to do when she got home. During spring and summer, we hung out in front of the building; it was pretty much the only option. We had to be within a call or earshot of my mother's voice; she needed to look out the window from the third floor and see us playing in the schoolyard or sitting on the school steps across the street. He wasn't hard to miss whenever he went to the corner store or ran an errand for his mother.

I thought he was cute. He was a good dancer at house parties, and he dressed pretty fly. He usually had the latest haircut, like the gumby, similar to the one that Big Daddy Kane sported. Or he would have a flat top, like Kid of Kid 'N Play, but his wasn't as high as Kid's. He was born in America, to parents who were from Antigua and the Virgin Islands, so we had one thing in common, Caribbean blood. I loved when we kissed. I really thought he kissed my heart, not my lips. I suppose that young love is supposed to pull on your heartstrings. Well, he certainly tugged on mine. We had so many conversations. We went to the movies, to my high school prom, we chilled on the block, he came to family events, my sweet sixteen, and I thought he was the one. I spent more time with him than I did with anyone else and by the time I was eighteen, I was ready. There had been times when we got close, but I just wasn't ready. He never pressured me, but we certainly talked about it on several occasions.

Other girls were attracted to all his physical attributes. I was taught at an early age that the outer shell—looks—are superficial and that they fade. It was really about how he treated me, at least in the early stages of our dating. I later learned that he had eyes for at least two of my cousins, but they never said anything to me. I guess publicly embarrassing me was the plan.

~ ~ ~

With just weeks left in my first year in college, I was sitting in a nurse's office. The wait was unbearable. I listened for every footstep, thinking the nurse had returned. I looked for the doorknob to turn with news of my results, but I had to wait. I was so nervous but hopeful that everything was OK. Being pregnant was the last thing on my mind. The nurse finally came into the room, and as I listened to her I was trying to figure out what I was going to say to my mother. The nurse confirmed it: "You're pregnant." My heart sunk. I had a million thoughts. I kept hearing the words, "you're pregnant" over and over again in my mind. The nurse saw how distraught I was. "I took the test twice, and the results were the same. You're pregnant," she said again. So that explained why I hadn't had my period in two months, even though it had been irregular anyway. I didn't think of going to see a nurse until my friends encouraged me to do so.

Reluctantly, I did, having no idea what she might say. I sat and started thinking about what I was going to do now.

What am I going to do about school? How will I tell my mother? What will other students think of me? Could I return to school? These questions rushed through my mind as the nurse began telling me about my options. There were two. She said, "You could go home and have the baby, or, here is your other option." And with that, she handed me some papers. She tried to comfort me and explained that I wasn't the only one who ever had to choose. She told me to take some time to consider those options.

As I left, each step I took felt heavier than the last. Suddenly, my dorm room was far away, not three buildings from the nurse's office. My heart was beating so fast and hard, I felt it in my throat. I finally got to my room, and I sobbed, hoping that my roommate wouldn't walk in. I didn't want to have to explain anything. At the time, I could not comprehend it myself. I was a first-year student in college. I was sexually active. Now I was pregnant. I was so scared. But even so, I knew I was not going to take that second option. At the time, I believed it was a woman's right to choose, but I also thought that I literally was going to hell. I was going to a fiery hell—the one where you're living on Earth—and burn because I had sex and got pregnant out of wedlock. I talked with a few really close college friends and asked them what I should do. I remember sitting in one of the other dorms, and we were trying to decide what to do as if it was our decision and not my decision.

When I first called my mom, I didn't exactly tell her that I was pregnant; I wanted to gauge her response. I told her a friend of mine got pregnant, and she didn't know what to do. Then my mother said, "Well, you know she probably shouldn't be having sex in the first place." My heart skipped another beat. It was near the end of the semester, and I had to go home. I had to tell her eventually, but I wanted to feel her wrath now before I got home because I knew she was going to let me have it. So, I told her over the phone. When we finished the conversation, I thought she was going to kill me.

"I sent you to school to get an education! I sent you to school so you can change your life! And now here you are getting pregnant? I can't believe you did this! I am disappointed!"

I thought her words were really harsh, but I knew they were the truth. A few weeks later, I packed up my room, and I knew it was my last time in this place. There are no babies here, and I didn't want to embarrass my friends or the reputation of the school.

Before I left, I wanted to inform the dean that I wouldn't return. His office was filled with baseball memorabilia and family photos that signaled to me he wouldn't understand. What looked like a husband and wife photo with smiling kids looked normal, contrary to the conversation I was about to have. After all, I was supposed to have children the traditional way—in my thirties, after I had established a career.

I sat with tears rolling down my face. I explained what was happening. I thought, what does this white guy really know about a girl from the Bronx getting pregnant? I was taken aback by his response. He reassured me that I could return when I was ready, and I always had a family on campus. I thought he was saying those words out of pity, but I later learned he was a man of his word. Surprisingly, I didn't feel judged; he made me feel human.

Riding home, it felt like the longest car ride ever. A friend drove me. We talked about what I would say and what I would do if I got kicked out of the house. My head was spinning from so many thoughts. I just wanted to fall asleep and not think. I had never seen a pregnant girl in college. I certainly never saw one graduate from college, so I felt that it wasn't possible. I had seen pregnant girls in high school, but never in college.

I got home and walked through the door, not knowing what to expect. I thought I knew what my mom was going to say. But she waited until the next morning, and she told me this: "This is where we are now. You got to figure out what you're going to do. You're going to have a talk with the baby's father and figure out a plan. Did he tell his parents?"

She threw a lot of questions at me, but I didn't have any answers. I hadn't had a face-to-face conversation with the baby's father. I had called him on the phone before I came home, but I was so disappointed with his tone. He didn't have much to say. When I told him I was pregnant, he said, "Well, what are you going to do?" I thought, why isn't he saying what are *we* going to do? When I asked him what he wanted to do, there was nothing but silence. I recalled that he was rarely quiet, but now there was silence over the phone. In my mind, his silence meant that he did not want this child. He never said it, but the tone of his voice told me he didn't want this baby. When we finally met in person, his answer wasn't definitive.

I had a birthday, three months into my pregnancy. I had some appointments, and I wanted the father of my child to at least show interest in the appointments. He claimed he would come, but most of the time he didn't. He promised he would come with me to Lamaze classes, but he never came. In the first class, everyone else was partnered with someone, even if the other person was not a girlfriend or boyfriend. Some came with a mother or mother-in-law. I was embarrassed and ashamed. During the train ride after the class, when I was seven months along, I cried. I cried the entire time, all the way from downtown up to the last stop on the No. 5 train. I was devastated.

At times, the emotional anguish was unbearable. So I made a promise to myself: this would never happen again. I would never depend on someone to the point where I couldn't move forward. I had expected him to be there to support me, and he didn't show. I hoped he would change his mind and want to take responsibility for this baby. My hopes were not realized.

Still, I was depressed. I was just in a deep, cold hole, and I needed somebody. My mother had specifically told me, "Don't ask him for shit." She was fierce, and she didn't mince words. I rarely saw him, and I decided to do this on my own. He never tied my shoes. He didn't rub my belly. I knew he wasn't going to call, so I had to move on mentally and physically, which meant I could not see him, even the days I really wanted to.

His sister and I were friends. She would call, and I would talk to her. A few times she passed the phone to him, but emotionally, it was very difficult to hear his voice. I really wanted to just tell him, "Motherfucker, don't talk to me. I'm pregnant with your child, and you couldn't give a shit. Don't speak to me!" But I remained silent because I was too angry to argue. It takes time to heal from this kind of pain. Eventually, when I was about nine months, we rarely communicated, and I knew for sure the relationship was over. I became more independent, but I was still in such a state of mind that I could hardly think. I was in a daze. I would either walk to an appointment or take the bus. My mind felt chaotic, and I didn't know what to do.

At the doctor's office, sitting in the waiting room, I saw how they treated people like me. I just did not like the way the doctors spoke to the patients: it was condescending. I was on Medicaid, and they definitely treated me differently. Years later, when I had insurance through my employer, I was able to verify the disparate treatment.

There were some highlights during my pregnancy. Friends and family gave me a baby shower, and I received some wonderful, thoughtful gifts. I was grateful for that. My mom helped me as much as she could. She would tie my shoes, and she bought me clothes without my asking her. She gave me money. I was appreciative of her help; she had my back. Also, Lisa came with me to some appointments; it really made a difference to have a conversation with someone else while I waited.

When I went into labor, my mom couldn't be at the hospital because she had to work. She knew someone should be with me, so she told me to call the baby's father, and to my surprise, he came to the hospital. Except for when he left to run an errand, he was there almost the entire time of the fourteen hours of labor. I'll never forget it. There was excruciating pain. No epidural, but I got some pain medication through the IV. It wasn't enough, however, because I felt every contraction. When my mom got off work, she came to visit. Other people came, too, including Lisa. The baby's father was there to witness the final moments.

Chapter Four

Wind Beneath My Wings

It didn't seem like a big deal that I now had a child because I knew a lot of single mothers. I desperately wanted to finish my degree. I thought of transferring the credits I had earned and completing my degree in New York instead of returning for the fall semester. But school was no longer my priority: I had to take care of my child. She was born during the winter, just before Christmas. For the first two months, I stayed at home. God gave me a priceless gift I didn't know I needed. It wasn't wrapped neatly with a gold bow. It wasn't one of those gifts that a person could set aside for weeks and then decide to use or wear later. It wasn't a gift my friends could borrow and return. It wasn't a gift I could admire from a distance. Instead, it was a gift to remind me that I wasn't in control of my life.

I'd had the next eight years planned. Four years of undergraduate, teach in New York City, live in a nice apartment in Manhattan, and then graduate school. I would travel to Antigua and other countries and eventually marry a man who loved me, admired me, and had eyes for only me.

It was cold, and unless there was a doctor's appointment, I didn't want to be outside. Like any new mother, I was so afraid of doing the wrong thing. How do I really take care of this new life? I checked on her constantly to see if she was breathing. The doctors always talked about Sudden Infant Death Syndrome. I became obsessed with checking her breathing. I placed my finger below her nose if I couldn't see her stomach rise and fall. I was paranoid. I was a nervous wreck. What if I took a nap, and I didn't hear her? Maybe these were all normal experiences of new mothers, but I had no clue.

We didn't have much space, so I kept her crib next to my bed in the room I shared with my youngest sister, Sharon. When she cried at night, I had to get up. Sometimes my mother woke up, tapped me, and said, "Don't you hear the baby crying?" Sometimes I heard her cries, but my mother was so quick. I think she knew I had the baby blues.

After my mother left for work, I went back to sleep and slept some more until the baby started crying. I fed her, she went back to sleep, and I slept some more. Sleeping was so comforting because I didn't have to think. There were times that I ate, watched TV, and went back to bed. Getting in the shower was too much work. Just lifting the shirt over my head or taking off my sweat pants required energy I didn't have, so I slept some more. I didn't want to hear my mother quarrel about the chores that weren't done; I usually got out of the bed at least an hour before she arrived.

Two months after my daughter was born, it became evident that I needed money in my pocket. I had Medicaid and WIC, but they didn't cover train fare, laundry, personal hygiene products, and clothes. One of my friend's sisters, Julia, gave me two large trash bags of baby clothes; her daughter was born a year earlier. I didn't even have to ask. She knew my baby's father and I were not together, and she wanted to bless me with the items. I looked for work as a cashier, and during that time I started going out with two friends to learn a trade to earn money. They were in the construction field, and I picked up basic skills and made a few dollars occasionally. I didn't know how to build a room, but I could measure drywall, plaster, sand, and paint. It was backbreaking work, and although I didn't go every day, I was exhausted. I found a new respect for the workers I saw on

46

the skyscrapers in New York or on buildings I passed on my way to the train. They worked through extremely hot and cold temperatures daily. We were all trying to do the same thing: make ends meet and provide for our families.

I couldn't get the type of job I wanted with no degree. There was nothing like feeling inadequate and unable to support my own child. It wasn't long before I started working as a cashier, at two different locations. I left one job and walked to the next. I worked two jobs, which equaled one full-time job. It was the only thing I could do to support my baby and me. There were days that time stood still, and the clock at work didn't move fast enough; I couldn't wait to get home. I was so happy to see her at the end of my shift. By playing with her on the floor, I didn't have to stand on my feet. It didn't take too much to make her smile, and she had the cutest nose and dimples. My mother taught me what type of food to feed her, not what the doctors prescribed. Caribbean mothers have MDs in holistic remedies; they could care less what the "real" MDs suggested. I made her cornmeal porridge, cream of wheat, bush tea (lemongrass or soursop), oatmeal, and other solid foods from Antigua.

As the season changed and time passed, my mentor Ms. Murphy asked me if I was going back to school in the fall. I told her that wasn't an option for me at that time. I wanted to stay with my child. Who leaves an eight-month-old to pursue a degree in another state, six hours away? The thought of leaving her was unconscionable, and I believed I wouldn't be a good mother if I did. She had just started mumbling a few unintelligible words. She was sitting up, playing, crawling, eating solid foods, and greeting me at the door when I got home from work. When I dropped her off at the babysitter before I went to work, I couldn't wait to see her face when I got home. She had the brightest smile that lit up my heart. How could I leave her? How would my mother pay for her daycare? I didn't have any money, and my mother was already taking care of my sister Sharon who was about nine years old. I would not have been able to focus on school when half of my mind would still be in New York. I couldn't see how going back to school would work, so I decided it was best that I stayed home. But then, things changed.

As time got closer to the beginning of the new school year, I had to talk to my mother about how it would work—my opportunity to complete my degree. If I didn't have the conversation, I knew Murphy would call my mother; she knew this method worked when she had the audacity to call me while on vacation in Antigua. Her reminding me of the preenrollment program I "must" attend prior to the beginning of the school year was all she wanted. That meant I would enroll weeks before most students arrived.

It was best to have the conversation with my mother first. Without much thought, my mother decided that she would take care of my daughter. We had a process in place for emergencies. Each year, I got a notarized letter stating that my mother had the responsibility of taking care of my daughter. It was essential that she had the appropriate documentation to make both medical and educational decisions. I would be too far away in an emergency. Summers were different; home was the only place that made sense for me.

I returned to school in the fall, but with a heavy heart. I was still torn between pursuing a degree and taking care of my responsibility as a mother. Murphy explained my options with or without a degree. I made a list, but I didn't want to hear what a degree would do for me ten years in the future.

Nevertheless, I prepared for the trip back to Vermont; this degree better be worth it.

The Greyhound ride seemed longer than I recalled. Usually I recognized the same faces on the bus from the previous year but not this time. At each bus stop, I thought of a reason to ask the driver about the next bus going back to the city. I felt defeated, a migraine headache ensued, and I fell asleep.

I woke up at one of the rural stops, either upstate New York or Vermont. Again, I thought, what am I doing here? There were only a few black and brown folks on this bus, no one looked like me in the convenience stores on the fifteen-minute layover, and the smell of cows no longer reminded me of Antigua but the place holding me back from my daughter. I was rationalizing why I didn't want to leave NYC, but I took a deep breath and was more determined than ever to finish this degree as soon as possible.

Stepping on campus now felt different. I knew I wasn't like the other students, but the friends I made during my first year were there to welcome me with open arms. They didn't judge me or keep their distance as if my pregnancy had been a disease. They were more interested in how I was doing now that I was back in school. They wanted to see pictures. They asked how they could help. They offered me rides to New York City without asking me to contribute to gas fare or tolls. And they asked if I needed a lawyer to help get child support. Shit, why didn't I think of getting a lawyer? Maybe because I couldn't afford one, and her father claimed he was in school to become a paramedic; I didn't think the legal route was necessary. What the hell was I thinking? As the father of this child, I shouldn't have had to ask or beg him for support. I had been at my lowest point, a true nadir, now trying my best to get out. Begging wasn't an option. My mother said a few things that always stuck with me:

"God will provide.

Who doesn't pay the just, will pay the unjust.

You can do this by yourself. You don't need him."

I quickly learned that you do need someone, but not necessarily that person.

I called home a few times each week. Hearing her voice brought me to tears. I couldn't kiss her plump cheeks, dance with her, carry her on my back as a joy ride, or feed her. There were times I didn't want to call because I knew how painful it would be, but I didn't have a choice: it was time for a visit.

Lisa brought my daughter to visit a few months later. I missed her so. I went to the bus stop to pick them up. When the bus arrived, I tried to recognize a baby's ponytail among the passengers sitting on the bus. I waved to my sister through the tinted window who pointed to her lap, which meant my daughter fell asleep. The anticipation of holding her was too great, and I wanted the passengers to move swiftly off the bus. I finally saw Lisa holding her little hands. She stepped down off the bus, one step at a time, and then she walked toward me. I was speechless. I called out to her to continue to walk. At first, I don't think she recognized me for a few seconds. Maybe it was the voice she heard for nine months talking to her about my troubles, or maybe it was instinct, but she began taking steps towards me—one, two, three, four—a slight pause to catch her balance.

In my excitement, I just scooped her up in my arms and held her tight. I smelled her, kissed her neck, her cheeks, and caressed every part of her body. I almost forgot that Lisa was there. This wasn't possible. A few months prior, she wasn't walking. She would stand up and hold onto whatever was nearby, but she certainly was not taking serious steps. As much as I loved to see her progress as a growing child, I was mad as hell I didn't see her first steps. I began to question and doubt my decision to return to school.

My friends knew she was my daughter, but others thought she was my little sister. I didn't want to have to explain to yet another privileged person that it was supposed to be my third year in college, but it was my sophomore year and that I took a year off to have a baby. Yes, I was a single parent, so don't ask me, "Is her dad a student here?" Or don't say, "Her dad must be so excited." Or don't pat her on the head; she's not a dog. Or "how cute is this?" She has a name, I thought, and there's nothing cute about doing this alone. It's interesting how we make assumptions about children, and what's considered the norm.

Now, the first spring break was a no-brainer. I stayed home. I didn't go to Cancun, the Bahamas, or to any of the great places some of my college friends were traveling. My priorities had shifted. It was such an accomplishment to end my second year. I didn't fail my classes. I studied as much as I could. Classes distracted my constant thoughts of being in

New York, and I had to convince myself and remember Murphy's words that this would all be worth it.

I didn't know how, but I had to do something other than standing on my feet as a cashier or plastering and sanding someone else's apartment when I didn't have my own. I felt triumphant and I started counting down. Two more years to go.

Chapter Five

Haunting Memories

The schoolwork became more challenging, and I was ignorant to the fact that history majors had to write two theses to graduate. As much as I loved learning about history and current affairs in Latin America and the Caribbean, the amount of work I had to do was daunting. I didn't have many intensive writing classes in high school. Our focus was on resistors, voltage, and math. Writing in college was extremely difficult, but using the writing center, spending hours in the library, talking with professors, and writing outlines and drafts before the final submission were lifesavers.

It was fascinating to learn that revolution was in my DNA. It's who I am. Whether I was acknowledging the relevance of Che Guevara, analyzing how the richest country in the western hemisphere gave birth to the revolutionary Toussaint Louverture, the origins of Carnival, the work of Rigoberta Menchu, or my Antiguan literary genius Jamaica Kincaid, I loved going to class. Yes, there were days when I couldn't read one more article, research another journal, or find something on microfiche, but what I learned far outweighed the anguish.

Small group discussions were my favorite because we had a chance to hear what other classmates thought, especially when we discussed the Caribbean. Facts are facts. But cultural experiences and student engagement are always different from what you read in a book or a journal. The college president taught one of my history classes, and he also lived a few houses away from the multicultural house where I lived. I wanted to make sure I paid attention for fear that when we asked for extra wood for the fireplace, he might recall that I was in his class. I was sure he had no clue, but the idea kept me focused.

I was so happy whenever we had a break. I either shared a car, or I took the long six-hour ride to New York City on the Greyhound. The bus wasn't the shortest trip, but I was able to read for my classes, take notes for an assignment, or figure out my plans before getting to the city. I fell asleep a few times and during one trip dreamed of a life that had once seemed impossible. In the dream, my daughter wasn't yet a teenager. She was running around in a backyard with other kids, and as I watched her, she seemed happy. I was suddenly awakened by the abrupt stop of the bus, and I was pissed. I wanted more of the dream. Where were we? Whose yard was it? Did I have a home? Damn bus! But aside from the dream, one plan remained: I was spending time with my baby girl.

On another break, I was so excited to finally take a friend home with me. This was a rare occasion because, culturally, we were taught to not invite company to the house. However, I invited only the three or four friends whom I trusted. On the ride from Vermont to NYC, I couldn't wait to show my friend the city, the bright lights, the legendary Bronx, and all things New York.

That magic I felt came to a halt after I opened the door to my house and was greeted by cold and hot air at the same time. The house was warm, but there was an obvious cold draft. The windows were misty, dripping with condensation. The curtains stuck to the windows because they were wet, and the plastic on the furniture was colder than usual. As my daughter ran toward me, I noticed that she was fully dressed, as if they were leaving the house. I wrapped my arms around her and closed my eyes to savor every moment of that. Then I noticed her nose was cold. When I opened my eyes, I saw the buildup of mildew in the left corner of the living room. I thought, doesn't mold make you sick? But I was distracted by my little angel leading me to play. She was happy, and my heart was warm, but as I continued walking into the dining room, I noticed the smell of heat. It sounds strange, but heat from the oven has a smell. All four burners on the stove were set on high, with big pots on them and steam everywhere. The oven door was open. This was one way to have heat when there was no oil in the tank.

My mother and father were not living together. They both came to the U.S. to pursue the American dream, but eventually with jealous family members and the lack of marriage counseling, the marriage fell apart. To my knowledge, he paid for the oil. But while I was away at school, something changed. I don't pretend to know everything that happened, but at some point, he stopped paying. Maybe I was dreaming, but the last time I checked, there was a toddler who happened to be his first granddaughter and his nine-year-old who lived in the house. I guess he didn't just forget to pay, he also forgot his humanity.

I couldn't believe what I was seeing and feeling. No oil meant no hot water and no heat. I can improvise with family; we know how to struggle and feed a family with limited resources. But how would my friend take a shower, wash her hair, or do anything else? I explained to her in brief details what was happening, and we made it work. That night, we played with my daughter and my sister until it was bedtime. I talked with my mom, washed the essentials, dressed, and fell asleep. The next morning, I took my classmate to my mother's friend's house to shower. We didn't discuss the incident after that day, and she didn't ask.

She didn't complain, but I was embarrassed. Not for my friend, but for my mother. This was a woman who had so much pride. Rarely, if ever, did she ask for help. And now she had two young kids in a cold house. She didn't call me at school to explain the issue before I got home; she knew it would be a distraction. Instead, she improvised with space heaters, simple baths, full clothing, open oven, and burners with pots to create steam. I thought it was dangerously genius, but what is a maid and single woman living in NYC to do? This happened once or twice, and it left an indelible imprint on what having heat meant. It was a reminder to me that the person who controls the money, controls everything else. I returned to campus to my heated room, contemplating how I could help to provide heat. But the pennies earned from my work-study job wouldn't make a dent in the cost of the oil. I thought of them being cold, suffering, wearing gloves and scarves inside the house, but I knew it was only my imagination. I convinced myself it was my imagination. In my mind, it meant that someone else controlled how much heat I had, or if I had heat at all.

To this day, I would spend my last dollar on heat. I refuse to be cold. As I thought about those moments, I was so angry with my dad for thinking he could do this, not only to the mother of his children but to his own flesh and blood. How will a nine-year-old function in school when she's trying to stay warm every night for God knows how long? My daughter probably had no idea. Children seem to adapt to the environment, and for all she knew, it was the tropics in that house.

Chapter Six

Light at the End of the Tunnel

By the end of my junior year, my mother and I could no longer afford childcare. She just didn't have the money. I was in college, and resources were limited. The only option at that point was to take my daughter to Antigua for a few months until I could find resources, or pray for a miracle. I spoke with my mom and also my aunt who lived in Antigua. We all thought it was the best choice, temporarily. But could I really do that? Could I leave my daughter in another country?

This was yet another major decision I had to make. Interestingly, my own parents had left me and my sister Lisa to pursue their American dream. Was I repeating a cycle of what my parents had done? I thought I understood it at the time, but I recall the loss and uncertainty of life when they left. Lisa and I were essentially reared by our grandparents and our aunt. They were the best surrogates any child could ask for. How do I really leave this child for any length of time with this feeling that I've abandoned her yet again? There was no easy answer again.

I went to Antigua with my daughter and my college classmate Evonne for about a week, but I knew my three-year-old would not return with us. I dreaded the passing of each day, and before I knew it, the week was over. My little daughter slept in the middle of my grandmother's bed. My heart broke as she slept, knowing that she wouldn't see me when she awoke. Was this the right decision? Was this something I would regret? Was I being selfish? So many questions flooded my mind.

Yet another thought entered my mind—that I should stay home from school, and work. I felt anxious. I was what I thought was the epitome of a bad parent. I questioned why I placed her in that situation. Yes, education was important, in fact, very important. But was it more important than taking care of this angel in this moment? I prayed incessantly, and then I unwillingly complied with my conscience. However, I vowed to never do this again. I would never leave her in another country where I wouldn't be able to visit regularly. I wondered if she would be traumatized. Logically, I understood why I had to do it, but I left in tears. Evonne did her best to comfort and encourage me, but it was a quiet plane ride back to the U.S. I worked feverishly that summer, and needless to say, I picked her up four months later. She had an Antiguan accent, and I worried that she would be teased in school.

Thank goodness it was my senior year; it couldn't come soon enough. I was ready for this chapter of my life to be over. Being broke, studying for hours without knowing where it would lead, traveling several times a year to the city, and missing pivotal moments in the life of my little girl all reminded me, again, how broke I was. It was time for a new beginning.

I desperately wanted to graduate in four years, so I enrolled in the Summer Immersion Language Program to gain additional credit hours and to fulfill the language requirement I needed to graduate. I learned so much that summer. There was nothing like being focused on one topic, and I was completely engaged. Students in the program weren't allowed to speak English after the first two weeks. The program was regimented, and the language school took learning and teaching seriously. We had a commitment ceremony and vowed not to speak English after two weeks.

We were all assigned a *madrina*—a godmother—to help us if we had questions. I met nontraditional students, some of whom claimed that they worked for the government and that they needed to learn the language for work. Maybe they thought that being in the mountains of New England was the best place to learn.

I was in beast mode. I worked out on a regular basis, and I started watching Spanish telenovelas to help with my listening skills. There was homework every day, and when we had parties, they were either in Spanish or in the language of the school that hosted the party. If students were caught not following the rules, they would get a warning, and I think after a second warning, the student was released. Discipline, collaboration, and laser focus in a controlled environment was just what I needed.

I made sure I passed all my classes as I mentally prepared for graduation. Students, of course, cannot walk across the stage and receive a diploma unless they successfully complete all courses. I checked with the dean's office on more than one occasion, and I knew exactly what I needed to graduate. I became obsessed with checking my grades and rewriting and reviewing papers like never before. I rarely skipped a class, and I'd have to be on my deathbed to miss one. There were days in which I had horrible menstrual cramps. Those were the only days I didn't attend classes. I simply had too much to lose. I couldn't call home to say that I needed more time because I didn't work hard enough, or that I didn't study effectively, or that I socialized to the point of failure. As a first-generation college student, there was no explanation for a lack of work. Most parents, including my mother, believed that there was nothing a student needed to do except study and go to class. Parties and social activities were optional, and as a matter of fact, they shouldn't be considered. I was there to work and nothing else.

Well in advance of graduation day, my mother knew she had to save money for the round-trip bus fare for her and my daughter. Money for food and lodging wasn't necessary. They stayed in my room. Since I lived in the multicultural house, we could use the kitchen; there was always food in the house. My village was my family.

Ordering and picking up my cap and gown, the senior bonfire, late nights at one of the favorite college pubs, applying to graduate school—these life-changing moments made it all so real. This was really happening. I don't know if

I asked permission, but I wanted my daughter to walk across the stage with me. There was a white graduation gown my sister Sharon had worn for her kindergarten graduation, and I asked my mother to bring it with her. We were both graduating that day and no one—not even the president—was going to tell me that I couldn't cross the stage with her. She was the only reason I did this and nothing else mattered.

We all got dressed that morning. There were a lot of well-wishes from my friends with whom I spent the last four years. Even as we were being seated, I still couldn't believe I was there. It was like an out-of-body experience. I knew that even if my daughter wouldn't remember, the pictures would tell a thousand words.

My name was called. I froze. Was it really my name? Maybe they made a mistake. My inner voice and the ancestors said, "Snap out of it! Carol, you've got it! Get up!" I held my daughter's little hands; I walked carefully onto the stage with my light brown, box braids, and my mortarboard was adorned with the Antiguan flag. As they handed me my diploma, a wave of emotions came over me, but it wasn't the time to break down, to faint, or to stumble on stage. I kept my composure. I shook the president's hand, and I kept walking back to my seat, where I embraced my mother. Her support was everything. We celebrated the rest of the afternoon before I took them to the bus stop for their ride back to the city.

That evening, I called my grandmother, and for the first time, I couldn't hold back the tears anymore. It was a bad cry. It was the type of cry where I couldn't catch my breath. The pillowcase was almost soaked, mucus running past my lips. It was almost impossible to formulate a sentence, and I felt like I had a fever. She kept asking me what was wrong, but I couldn't speak. Then finally, I was able to tell her that I graduated. I thanked her for the prayers, for loving me unconditionally, and for the wisdom to know when God is in control.

My grandmother was a praying woman. She taught me how to pray. Sometimes the prayer was "Help me, Lord Jesus." I know most of the Psalms because of her and going to church a few days a week. I honestly didn't know if I could graduate. Yes, I was determined. I worked hard. I was distracted many times, but I made it. I now had my degree in hand, written in Latin. I was so elated. There were family members who had snickered and believed it wasn't going to happen, but this was not about them. I wanted a different future for my daughter. My mentor, Murphy, told me this was the first step in changing my life, and she was right.

By then, I had applied to and was admitted to graduate school. Although this was something I knew nothing about, I believed I could accomplish that too. After all, I just did the impossible.

My friends and my village were phenomenal. They helped me take care of my daughter when she visited during our winter term. She stayed for the entire month of January for three consecutive years. We had one class during the month of January, and of course, someone had to babysit each year. My village took turns watching her for a few hours at a time. A special man was also part of the village. I had no idea how special he would be. They all stepped up when I needed them the most. There were times when I didn't have extra food, and since we lived in a house, we cooked and pooled our resources. When I didn't have disposable diapers, they helped. My village always asked before going to the supermarket if I needed anything, and I couldn't lie to them. They also bought a few toys to keep her happy.

I recall not being able to buy up an entire pack of diapers; in New York City we had what we refer to as "loosies" or items in one pack sold individually. For example, we have loosie cigarettes; you didn't have to buy the whole pack if you couldn't afford it. Although the brand name diapers were popular, most of the times I couldn't afford them. It was interesting when, years later, I was attending an event at one university that featured the CEO of Procter & Gamble, the makers of the very diapers that I couldn't afford years ago. I felt that God was talking to me in that moment. *Look how far you've come!* I was quiet for awhile, and then the feeling of gratitude came over me. It was a student event, so I had to keep my emotions in check because this event was not about me. But I do remember feeling and thinking that God loves me. There was a path created for me because of His love, mercy, and grace. It was really a moment of reflection and feeling beyond blessed. Sometimes you just have to sit in silence and think about God's favor.

Chapter Seven

God's Plan

Students can become our best teachers. While I completed my teaching practicum for my license to teach grades 7–12, I quickly learned that some middle school students had little to no interest in social studies. Between their reaching puberty and having social development issues, I suppose there was no room for Harry S. Truman or for the Aborigines. This age group wanted and needed a sounding board and a listening ear. I didn't know how to respond. As a soon-to-be teacher, I didn't recall theory and practice classes to address these concerns. I wanted to make a bigger impact on the lives of students.

It first came in the form of a silent protest in the university president's office. Both undergraduate and graduate students banded together and devised a list of demands for the institution. Our demands included increasing the number of black students and faculty there. When we congregated upon the president's office, I realized the power of the students' voices. But it was hot in that room with so many people, and wearing my green sweater didn't help. We sat on the floor and refused to leave unless we were heard. Students who attended classes took notes for those who didn't. The media or some other company offered food to us, and I certainly didn't go to classes most of the day. I knew this could have a negative impact on my grades and career, but at the time, fighting for the future of students seemed more important. I wish I knew then what I know now. We should have suggested a systematic, sustainable plan that monitored progress yearly to hold the administration accountable.

Whatever plans I had for my teacher's license, God had another plan for me: college students. After I completed my master's in teaching, and as I waited for that special man who would become my boo thang to complete his doctorate in chemistry, there was an opportunity for me to become a graduate assistant, to recruit and retain graduate students. I decided to pursue a master's in counseling. The courses in this program were needed for middle school students as well. I also thought that I could use these skills in the future— skills such as active listening, group dynamics, connecting with others, and advocating on their behalf when needed.

However, being genuine and the ability to empathize have been the skills that have taken me the furthest in my career.

Within two years of graduate school, I was asked to redesign a program to help undergraduate students acclimate to campus life. I went to my supervisor in tears because I loved the job I already had. I expected him to be aggravated as he needed to hire my replacement. It was the first professional job that I had to leave, and I really did not want to. It was serendipitous; he was elated and explained that this is what happens when you do good work: others will see your gifts. He wished me well and offered to help with my transition any way he could. I recall thinking that when I become someone's supervisor, I was going to be happy when they moved on to bigger and better opportunities. This is what leadership looks like.

A few months later, I officially started my career as an academic advisor. It was absolutely rewarding, and I wouldn't change it for anything. I could share strategies to succeed and lessons I learned from my own experience, to make sure students were on track to graduate.

Quite often, parents, teachers, counselors, and community members think of professors and administrators when they consider the students' experience. However, advisors are some of the major contributors to student retention and success. Parents and students don't realize that if they meet with their advisor once per term, not only are they increasing their chances of graduating within four years but they will save money in the process. Advisors are educators, unofficial social workers, therapists, and sometimes pseudo-parents; they can be the difference between enrollment and graduation.

In my opinion, academic advising is one of the most undervalued and underpaid positions in higher education. Many, if not most, advisors are not part of a union. If they only knew the collaborative power they have as a group, they could bring every university to their knees. Sometimes, it takes one voice to send shockwaves throughout the advising world; the time is now. Imagine if there was an all-advising strike around the country to improve wages and create more career paths. Revolution is in my blood, but I digress.

Just as important, the people with whom I worked were a really good advising team. We talked about everything, and I mean everything, imaginable. I wish I could bottle up that experience and let other advising units know how to build strong and lasting relationships that work. It wasn't perfect, but we worked diligently to cultivate the relationship early enough to have those crucial conversations about race, intersectionality, gender, and sexuality. Most questions were not off-limits, and as a result, they knew not to touch my hair—enough said. We grew professionally and personally.

It took a few years, but I was able to have similar relationships at my new job in another state. I loved and missed the times we had between appointments, singing Tina Turner, gospel music, the *Hawaii Five-O* theme song, and other tunes. Building relationships with teammates is key, but first there must be trust. When trust is broken, there's no turning back.

I have worked on one personal challenge each year, whether it was being nicer, being more patient, or what Martin Luther King Jr. called "sincere ignorance and conscientious stupidity." Needless to say, I didn't master having more patience with incompetence. I'm no longer working on that challenge.

Trying to balance my personal and professional life wasn't what I thought. Why did I think there was a switch that turned off because I was at home? There were dishes, laundry, cleaning, and childcare to take care of. Of course, it was difficult to shut off my brain, especially if there were students who needed additional support. Not having family nearby is worse when you begin a new job. I lived four hours away from my mother and sister, so I couldn't stop by for dinner, or if I was too tired to cook, or if I needed help with childcare.

It has been fourteen years since my transition to Cincinnati, and some days I question my cultural adjustment. It's different from the East Coast; I guess I'm used to people being more overt. In New York City, if someone doesn't like you, you know it and feel it. Why is it so much work to figure it out here? I stopped trying.

Before we could buy our first home, we had to get a loan. They drew up all the paperwork at the bank, but when the documents were finally sent to us, to them we were categorized as being white. I had no idea how this happened. I know we didn't tell them we were white as all the transactions occurred by phone. My husband spoke with them; I didn't want my accent to be the reason we didn't get the loan. I live in America.

We were finally able to look at a few homes we saw online. The Realtor took us to one home on the other side of town. Based on our online research, the neighborhood had great schools, people looked friendly, families seemed to congregate, easy access to the highway, shopping centers nearby, and about thirty minutes from work. We pulled up to the house, and it was exactly what we thought, except for the Sambo statue at the back of the house. This particular Sambo was a stereotypical, lazy, black man, dressed in a yellow shirt, red hat, bulging eyes, sitting with a big smile—the only thing missing was the watermelon. That was the only thing I needed to see; the house was off my list. Since the Realtor was a few steps away from my loud, Caribbean mouth, I gently told my husband I would wait in the car. I had no plans to give the homeowners any business. My husband had more patience than I. He continued the tour of the house, and they met me in the car. It was a warm summer day, and I'm sure the house had air conditioning, but I refused to be part of this lack of sensitivity for any homebuyer. I'm sure they didn't know a black, conscientious couple would be potential buyers.

A few years later, we applied for a refinance loan. We talked on the phone and were approved. The only thing left to do was sign the paperwork. We got to the bank, and we were literally about to sign, and then they told us we weren't approved. I was furious, and my husband knew it. I wasn't optimistic about the city, but I knew there was no turning back; we already signed on the dotted line to build a life in Cincinnati.

Acclimation to this new environment was challenging, to say the least. I was lonely. I missed my mother and sisters dearly. They were now almost eleven driving hours away, or two hours by plane, plus another thirty minutes to get to Harlem. Family members are always important, but I felt it more when I was farther away. Traveling back and forth had become more strenuous. FaceTime wasn't initially an option. And I owned a house, not an apartment. There was more work to do as a homeowner.

Chapter Eight

It's Social Justice

I have been affectionately called "Momma Mack," "Dean Mack," and "Ms. Mack." They may call me other names, but they haven't been bold enough to say them to my face. I tell most of my students that I am not here to be liked, but that I'm here to make sure they walk across the stage and get that degree. Students are perplexed when I am happy to see them leave. I then have to explain that they've accomplished an important goal: graduation.

My students mean the world to me. I will advocate for them by any means necessary. Isn't that what all parents want when they send their children to live among complete strangers? If a student is having issues, I will make a phone call or visit someone's office to make sure the student's voice is heard. There is a fine line between asking students to become independent human beings and asking them to navigate the sometimes treacherous waters of higher education. There is a new, unfamiliar vocabulary in every college office that we expect them to know and understand after the first semester; this is impossible. Like any foreign language, it takes time. Moreover, first generation college students have a completely different experience.

In my experience, students appreciate when I take the extra step to help meet their needs. I've heard the critics say this is hand-holding, but it really isn't. For me, it's about social justice.

I recall a few years ago when a professor didn't respond after a student sent multiple emails. The student was concerned about his grade and needed guidance to improve in the class. I asked him to show me the emails he sent. After visiting the professor's office, I quickly realized that he wasn't ignoring the student. He never received the student's emails. His approach in scheduling appointments was somewhat archaic; he didn't use modern technology. Students had to sign up on his door for an appointment. Simply walking over to the professor's office was an easy way to resolve the issue.

Ask yourself: wouldn't you want an advocate if your child, brother, or sister had a similar issue? If there's a legal issue, we have lawyers; the sports world has agents; college students need advocates. I'm always reminding students that some professors are not trained teachers; many are researchers. They are paid to do research, publish papers, and give service to the department and university; teaching is one small part of the pie at research institutions.

In my twenty years of working with students, I have never been disappointed. I may not have liked a particular decision, but I have become more disappointed in the unjust system that plagues education at all levels. For example, we continue to use test scores and other arbitrary criteria that become barriers that keep some students out. There are hundreds of universities that are test-optional, why not all?

Every parent or guardian wants a return on his/her investment. I don't know why more parents aren't more intrusive. Call it being a "helicopter parent" or a "Black Hawk parent," but we all need someone to watch over us. I have always firmly expressed that there's nothing wrong with a helicopter parent. It's how close that parent hovers that can become problematic. Yes, students have rights, and as parents we must teach them to ask the right questions. But how do we know which questions are "right" when higher education is a culture in and of itself?

There once was a student who convinced his parents that he would graduate, when in fact he would not graduate.

They reserved the hotel, booked the flight, and made dinner reservations to celebrate his graduation that wasn't going to happen. Those parents had paid his rent for years, but they never really checked to see if he was actually graduating.

We don't expect our children to tell boldface lies, but often times they don't want to disappoint us or not live up to our expectations and dreams. University officials are bound by confidentiality. Students must give permission to release certain information to a parent or guardian. You better believe that when my daughter attended college, I had permission for financial aid, academics, and residential matters. However, I forgot to get permission for health insurance until it was too late. It wasn't a question of *if* she wanted to give permission but *when* she planned to add me to the list. I teach my children to first ask for help, send an email, but if needed, visit the professor or the financial aid office. However, after a few attempts without resolution, I will step forward and demonstrate to them how it's done. They need to know how to handle similar issues the next time; it teaches them problem-solving skills.

Essential skills must be taught, such as balancing your account, posting a letter, depositing a check, and making your own doctor and dentist appointments. I know there's so much we do online, but if you don't know the basics, and the technological systems are down, what do you do then?

Many students attend college, but they're not ready. At times, parents want their children to attend certain schools out of loyalty, legacy, or lunacy. How on God's green earth will a child really succeed if they don't want to be there in the first place? I've learned over the span of my career that it's possible for even the most intelligent of students to fail classes. Not because they don't know the material, but because for the first time in their lives, they must study, manage their time, stay focused, and become in-depth learners. The first C, D, or F grades they receive can be devastating to students; the arena is more competitive, and they're no longer top of the class. This can be extremely depressing, and it can deeply impact that student's life, emotionally and mentally.

In my advising role, I've asked students on numerous occasions: besides finances, what's the biggest college challenge? The answers are always the same: time management and not enough time to comprehend the amount of material for different classes.

For this reason, utilizing academic resources should be mandatory, specifically for courses in which they earn poor grades. This is due in part to the majors that the students select. Are we really expecting students in their late teens to make the "right" decision about majors and careers? Didn't we all learn that the brain doesn't fully develop until the early twenties? When I informally polled parents, at least eight out of ten were not pursuing a career directly related with their college major. Nonetheless, many wanted their children to major in business or the sciences. Liberal arts majors are, at times, the last choice.

People tend to underestimate the value of a liberal arts education. However, many community organizers, leaders in education, and leaders in the private sector obtained liberal arts degrees. Yet some of us are fixated on our children completing a Science, Technology, Engineering, and Math (STEM) degree.

First of all, college isn't for all students, but all students should contribute to the community; maybe that means a certificate or vocation. For those who decide to go the science and technology route, they may have been a STEM rock star in high school, but in college some of them feel like a novice, even after taking AP courses. AP courses in high school are different from college courses taught on campus by the professor who may have written the textbook.

My job is to tell students the truth. To ask them why, to help them set goals, challenge, and motivate them to get to the next level.

One of my students had a difficult time with grades after her first year, and she cried profusely. I passed the tissues. I gave her the time and mental space she needed to cry. Sometimes, that's all students need. I sat with her in silence until she was ready to listen and devised a plan to move forward. She reminded me years later of this meeting, and we laughed. She simply thanked me for listening and mentioned that my firm but gentle attitude encouraged her to be successful. She is now a proud alumna and is currently enrolled in a professional school.

Never forget the adage: treat others as you would like to be treated. We should actively listen to students and help open their minds to the possibilities. When they develop a strong connection with us, this is when the real work begins—figuring out the next steps. Although we can't or shouldn't make the final decision for students, we can certainly help guide the process, whether academically or personally.

For students with low self-confidence and low self-esteem, depending on the circumstances, I try to remind them that they're smart, special, deserve to be here, and have the ability to succeed. I ask that they make a few Post-it notes, place them on the bathroom or bedroom mirror, and have a self-talk each day or a few days per week. The notes must be positive: I am worthy. I will get through this. He/she lost a good thing. Success is the best revenge. This is only a setback.

I don't know if they actually do this ritual, but I hope they realize that, more than anything else, I support them and will be their best personal cheerleader.

There were a handful of women who listened, encouraged, pushed, and motivated me during my undergraduate and graduate years, whether it was Murphy, Clookey, Helen, Mrs. V., or others. It is now incumbent upon me to pay it forward. After all, when you educate a child, you change the trajectory of not only the family but perhaps an entire community.

I am honored to receive the invitations to graduation dinners, parties—and weddings are my favorite. To watch the personal and professional growth of students who become alumni warms my heart. This is really when I get my conscience paycheck.

I truly believe that my students may one day become my doctor, lawyer, colleague, neighbor, pharmacist, or manager at my local supermarket. We must be kind to our students because we never know when they're going to sit across from us in a boardroom, making decisions about whether we should be hired for that new position. It's not preposterous to think that students could be our future employers. We taught them the skills to succeed. We should want those skills to be used with us in mind.

Chapter Nine

The Man. The Mission. The Magic.

He loves me. He tells me he loves me every day, and we never go to sleep without resolving an issue. With his personality, in his head he may have moved on from the topic, but he knows I must hear words and not imagine them.

He respects me. Unless a man respects you, he will not accept a child that's not his biologically, nor give her his last name, nor treat her as if she were his own. My mother instilled in me that a man should accept the cow and the calf; if not, keep it moving. I don't know where she comes up with these colloquialisms. My daughter adores him. You should see her Facebook postings each year on his birthday and on Father's Day!

He is a great father. Despite his other administrative duties, research, and other responsibilities, he makes time for homework with our children. We split the duties. I take care of English and social studies; he takes care of math and science. He is very patient with his explanations, and he will repeat the example, as many times as necessary, to make sure they understand the information. Sometimes the tasks are not complete until after midnight. Still, he will answer emails and complete other work tasks that were not finished during the day.

He can't fix everything. I always tease him. He thinks he's black Jesus. In our house, we have a picture of the last supper with black Jesus and his disciples. So every time he tries to fix yet another problem at work, I always remind him that he's not black Jesus; he really can't save them all.

He loves to travel with me. In 2016, we had our first Caribbean cruise, and we visited six different islands. We explored the Caribbean culture before we actually visited my native country in 2017. There's something about having little to no access to technology. He's an excellent planner and attentive to small details.

He gives me butterflies, twenty years later.
He is my personal Idris Elba; back up off him.

88

He's a mama's boy.

He wants to wear comfortable clothes to work, but he knows he will be perceived negatively.

He's too patient.

He's no pushover, except to his daughter.

He's a science geek.

He's the best organic chemist.

He will be dean.

He's a workaholic.

He's over-prepared for important meetings. Don't test him.

He thinks.

One of his favorite quotes (by Mike Tyson) is: "Everybody has a plan until they get hit."

He should have been a lawyer.

He has too many gray hairs for his age. It's genetic.

He is not immune to the conditions of being a black man in America.

He wears too many hats. It's time to give up at least one.

He believes he's Black Superman, son of Jor-El. I am not Lois Lane.

He is a stress-free husband. Literally, it takes an act of God to piss him off. I can't recall a time when he was frustrated at home, and I had no idea how to respond.

He's a provider like nobody's business. There was a time when our funds were more limited. We had a newborn, and I was skeptical how it would work since he was completing his post-doc. Childcare was so expensive. Nevertheless, the bills got paid. We never got any disconnection notices, even while we were paying two childcare bills. He made it seem as smooth as a baby's bottom.

He doesn't have a lot of friends. He doesn't have time, and he's not the kind who maintains constant, consistent communication with them.

He makes me tea. Yes, he makes me hot tea, with milk and sugar. Sometimes, it's not always the right amount of sugar. But when he brings it to me in bed, who cares?

#BlackManMagic.

My family photo in Antigua after confirmation. Left to right: Aunt Rosalie, Auntie Blandina, Hilda Pryce (grandmother), John Pryce (grandfather), Lisa, and me.

My confirmation photo, circa 1979.

My favorite baby photo: two years old.

My undergraduate graduation photo. Walking across the stage with my daughter.

One of my daughter's childhood photos, circa 1993.

2015 family photo.

Chapter Ten

The Darker the Flesh, the Deeper the Roots

In September of 2013, my career was disrupted. I was attending a college fair. At that point, I had been an assistant dean for two months. While at the fair, a colleague sent me an email and attached a cartoon. Copies of the cartoon were posted on bulletin boards, as flyers, at the university. The cartoon was a caricature of me, along with the dean. The cartoon depicted us both as dictators. The heading (italics added, spelling errors retained) read:

"Carol Tong & Ronald Jackson (self-appointed) King & Queen of A + S."

A + S means Arts and Sciences. I was drawn as a large black woman with huge girth. There was a crown on the caricature's head and a scepter in her right hand. She appeared to be angry. Wearing high heels, her left foot was planted firmly on the bleeding corpse of what students and others believed to be a white woman sprawled mercilessly on the floor. Blood seeped from the lifeless body. The first frame of that cartoon read:

"I am now the queen and Ronald the King! Screw the faculty and those who were here before us!"

The second panel of the cartoon was a close-up of the caricature that was supposedly me. The quotation in it was:

"Education will be secondary!! We will crush those who oppose us!!!"

The depiction of Dean Jackson first appeared in the third frame of the cartoon. He, too, appeared to be angry. His caricature was dressed in a suit and tie, but only the upper torso was shown. The quotation in it was:

"Cut off all faculty Communication. Cut out the employees that resist!"

In the fourth frame, Dean Jackson and I appeared together. Both caricatures, full figures, were standing. The caricature of Dean Jackson now wore a crown, and he was holding a briefcase. The caricature of myself was still holding the scepter in my right hand and still wearing the crown. The quotation read:

"Fire anyone that does not look like us! They have no rights!"

Finally, the fifth and last frame had a rectangular shape, whereas the previous four were all squares. Frame five

98

was the size of two of those squares. In that fifth frame, the silhouettes of four people were standing in the entrance of a large, open area. It appeared to be a wall, and its entrance was to the university campus. There were four quotes, one for each silhouetted person.

(Left top): *"All hail the self appointed King and Queen!"*
(Right top): *"How long until they destroy the University?"*
(Left bottom): *"Will we last!"*
(Right bottom): *"No we do the work that keeps A+S Functioning."*

There was a fifth quotation. It came from a rat that was also a silhouette, drawn in the foreground but near the bottom of the frame.

"I used to like it here! time to transfer!"

The cartoon's creator left a sort of moniker that read:

"StudentZ" Save A+S"

The Z in Student was drawn very large, sort of like the mark of Zorro. And finally, at the very bottom of the cartoon was this caption:

"Fight this new desease!!"

I was utterly disgusted by the entire cartoon, but the last statement was especially degrading. It truly felt like a slap in the face after all of the work, sweat, and sometimes tears. Am I really a disease? I showed the cartoon to my daughter and my son. It was so deeply painful. People asked me who was the white woman I was crushing. Of course I had no idea. I was so wrapped up in disbelief. It was the most powerless I ever felt in my life. I felt somewhat discombobulated. It reminded me of a quote by Malcolm X:

> The most disrespected person in America is the black woman.
>
> The most unprotected person in America is the black woman.
>
> The most neglected person in America is the black woman.

The media called, but I didn't respond. I knew I shouldn't say anything to the media. For the first time in my life, I didn't have words. I lost something that day. Actually, I did have words but they would have sabotaged my career. I had just completed a women's leadership program with the local chamber of commerce, and we discussed how women sometimes sabotage their personal lives and careers. So I thought it was in my best interest to not say much; it could have been a career-ending moment.

To my knowledge, no organized group approached the university administration and said that this behavior was unacceptable and that we cannot treat another woman on campus with such disrespect. The Lambda Society was the only formal group that reached out to me with kindness and support; I can always depend on my sisters. As a staff member, without a union, I did not have the same protection as faculty. But this was not the way the institution treats faculty or the way women are treated. Maybe deep down, I didn't expect support, but it would have been nice. Of course, I couldn't go to Dean Jackson. He, too, was going through the drama—the trauma—so we didn't talk about it much. Sadly, about two months later, under pressure from faculty and others, Dean Jackson resigned his position. And with that, it was the most isolated I have ever felt in my career.

I took a deep breath and sent a copy of the cartoon to an upper level administrator. Two colleagues from our marketing department walked around campus, searched for, and removed the flyers; I'm not sure if they found all copies. But it had become public. And when it became public, students called. They were trying to process it and understand. A female student wanted to know what this cartoon meant for her as a future leader. She asked, "If I get a promotion or anything else in my career that others disagree with, will they do this to me?" My simple answer was, "I don't know. I have no idea." I was literally holding back tears. She was asking questions I had not thought of at the time.

This was a much larger societal issue, and I was suddenly thrust into the insecurities, resentment, and resistance of others to say the least. What does this mean for other young black women and girls who want to pursue leadership roles? I was so distraught most days, I just did not know what to do, so I buried myself in work. It was the best way I knew to handle all of the emotions. Finally, I took a long overdue emotional break at the end of the semester. I spoke with the interim dean, and she told me to take as much time as I needed. I took ten days, but I needed more time than I thought.

I couldn't do anything at home. I struggled to get out of bed, and when it was time to return to work, I struggled to get there most days. At home, the only thing I did was clean because it was a stress reliever. I felt somewhat disconnected from my family. Thank God for my husband. He started doing the daily chores and held me up.

Eventually, I began counseling sessions to learn coping strategies. The sessions were extremely helpful. There's nothing like talking to someone who's completely objective and doesn't know all the players involved in this emotional game. The counselor was there to listen. She tried to comprehend. She provided critical feedback, and I had homework. The assignments were challenging, to say the least, and she held me accountable. I vowed after counseling that no woman, I don't care what she looks like, would ever have that experience again—that it would not happen under my watch.

I was so happy that my grandmother taught me how to pray. The book of Psalms and the book of Isaiah were and remain my good friends. Praying became a ritual for me. I could hear my grandmother's voice repeating the first verse of Isaiah, chapter 60: "Arise and shine, for your light has come and the glory of the Lord rises upon you."

I was ready to talk to my children about the incident. My son was twelve years old at the time. He couldn't handle the discussion, even if I used the simplest terms, so I figured we could revisit the topic as time passed. I would probably show him the cartoon before he left for college. I didn't want him to find it online while having no clue about it. My daughter, on the other hand, was a bit different; she was a senior at the same university. I thought she should know just in case someone approached her or had something to say. I explained the situation to her in detail and she said this: "Mommy, they are just haters." She returned to her room, and we no longer discussed it.

The university eventually published a statement about the cartoon, but most people had no idea to whom or what they were referring. Some students protested on campus, which also included reasons related to racial climate, and I loved them for that. They, too, wanted to be heard. Ironically, on the day of the protest, there was also an admissions event. I was expected to be there to meet prospective students, along with their parents. I had to tell them all how great the institution was. The assistant director and I were trying to decide how I should be introduced. We did not want to bring too much attention to or make people aware that I was somewhat connected to the protest outside.

The presentation was most difficult, but I put on a brave face and did my job. At the end, I felt like a hypocrite. The writer Paul Laurence Dunbar wrote:

> We wear the mask that grins and lies,
> It hides our cheeks and shades our eyes.
> This debt we pay to human guile;
> With torn and bleeding hearts we smile...
> We smile, but, O great Christ, our cries...
> We wear the mask... (Dunbar 1896)

My heart pounded because I wasn't true to myself. But I knew I had to take care of business. Those prospective students and parents in the room had nothing to do with whomever created and distributed that cartoon. They deserved to enjoy their visit without distraction.

~ ~ ~

Deeper Feelings Derived

What most people don't understand about black women, such as me, is this: we are not stupid. We see the games people play. We know exactly when others disapprove because some of us (me included) are not very good at hiding our feelings.

People's actions speak louder than words. We carefully observe everyone. We are learning how people treat others, and we're not expecting anyone to treat us differently. Many don't feel the need to know anything about us. The microaggressive behaviors you exhibit are very obvious, and they show up on a macro level. Whatever you're planning to do at work or in your position of power tomorrow or the near future, we already know your next move. Just like I saw you then, I see now.

The black woman who can go between several worlds—from Ebonics to patois, from standard English (whatever that means) to Ebonics, from the ghetto to the boardroom. Yes, I blur the lines often, but so do you; we're not taught to tell you when you're wrong. You just mad (that's right, there's no linking verb) because you cannot go through so many worlds in the matter of minutes. Ironically, you don't know how to stop me, so the only thing you can do is try to shut me down.

The attempts to make small talk and give compliments—when we already know our work speaks for itself—don't work. I see you. Your actions didn't surprise me, but now you smile and pretend it didn't happen. I had to ask permission to attend a professional presentation and specific meetings. Apparently, others were intimidated by my presence because I was in a higher administrative role.

This is all I care to share with the world so far. There's no going back to the way it was. I had to find a new normal. I clearly understand the ramifications and the direct results of hatred, disdain, and the like, for strong people of African descent. What is far more interesting at this juncture is who's considered worthy and whether or not black women's lives matter. There is so much more I could say about the cartoon and how it affected me.

The real ugliness of the person behind the cartoon was that this black woman was leading. Me. The boisterous, black woman whose laughter is described in Maya Angelou's poems. A couple of my thoughts were temporarily shut down, but I wasn't shut down permanently. Like a phoenix, I always rise from the ashes.

Chapter Eleven

"Your Crime Is Your Ignorance" —*attributed to Cicely Tyson*

To the coward who posted the flyers around campus:
You are a coward! You continue to hide behind the white
sheets of injustice and the despicable words of the cartoon. I
am almost certain your intentions were to smear my name
and remind me that I am not in my place. I know you prefer
that I am washing the dishes, cleaning your house, or serving
you in some capacity. My ancestors worked too hard for me
to be where I am today. Neither you nor anyone else can
remove me; it'll happen when God/Goddess is ready. You
got one thing right with the cartoon, the sketch portrayed me
with a crown because you knew I was a queen. James Baldwin
said, my crown has been bought and paid for, all I have to do,
is wear it.

I am wearing my crown! Yes, that's right. I deserve to be a queen. Initially, I had so many questions for you; however, I realized that you don't have permission to give me answers. You're not worth me listening to your negative responses or excuses. I've decided it's really: what should I do now that I know who you are? I may not know your first and last name, but I know that you represent oppression, hatred, inequality, and injustice. You are perturbed that I walk with purpose and exude confidence you wish you had. You're a bully, and your attempt to intimidate me will not work. No weapon formed against me shall prosper. I leave you with a gift by Maya Angelou:

> You may write me down in history
>
> With your bitter twisted lies
>
> You may trod me in the very dirt
>
> But still, like dust, I'll rise

Does my sassiness upset you?

Why are you beset with gloom?

'Cause I walk like I've got oil wells

Pumping in my living room...

Did you want to see me broken?

Bowed head and lowered eyes?

Shoulders falling down like teardrops,

Weakened by my soulful cries?

Does my haughtiness offend you?

Don't you take it awful hard

'Cause I laugh like I've got gold mines

Diggin' in my own backyard.

Out of the hugs of history's shame

I rise

Up from a past that's rooted in pain

I rise...

Bringing the gifts that my ancestors gave,

I am the dream and the hope of the slave.

I rise

I rise

I rise.

(Angelou 1978)

God has a way of teaching us timing. What if this occurred in my twenties when I didn't know how to react to this type of buffoonery? There were days I wished I was in the South Bronx on the corner of Manor and Watson with some of my friends and cousins; those days were survival of the fittest. My reaction to this bullshit would've been completely different. Most of my family members didn't know what happened with the cartoon, but my sister Lisa and mother knew. They were very worried and concerned for my safety; they had so many questions. I couldn't give them any clear answers, and I couldn't tell them the whole truth. Lisa, my mother, and some of my other family members would've probably been on the first plane or bus to Cincinnati. Trust me, you don't want them here. First, you wouldn't understand the patois language because when West Indians get pissed off, naturally our native tongue is the only language spoken.

Interestingly, I walked through crack vials, drug dealers, dirty old men, and others society frowns upon to get to high school in the South Bronx, and they were usually kind to me. Drug dealers usually said "Mommy, stay in school, don't be like me." This was almost on a weekly basis. They were always encouraging, but now I have "educated" people discouraging and disparaging me with their commentary and heinous cartoon.

I am reminded of one of my journal entries during that time. My son learned about Julius Caesar and how he was killed. As he explained, I asked what Julius Caesar did to deserve death. He said Caesar was popular, powerful, and he was successful. My son then proceeded to say, "Mommy, you and daddy don't want to be killed like him." My heart sunk. He thinks we're popular at work. I thought the analogy was profound, and I thought about it for days. Out of the mouth of babes!

Whenever there's a crisis, I internalize my thoughts, everything stays inside, and I try to make an illogical situation logical. I wanted to have a human response, but I knew it wasn't in my best interest to speak; what I had to say no one would've liked. Honestly, I did not want them to see my black rage, but it was there. The caricature in the first frame of the cartoon was given a crown to inspire ridicule and shame, but these healing words from Common the rapper came to mind:

"Even Jesus got his crown in front of a crowd."

Chapter Twelve

Life Lessons

Life is an ever-changing journey with no GPS, no instructions. We all want to believe life will work as planned because we either prayed incessantly, worked without taking a vacation, kept our homes as spotless as possible, or paid for the most prestigious private or parochial schools. We grow and learn from different experiences, and when it's least expected, pain comes before promise.

From the beaches in Antigua, the concrete jungle of the boogie down, the cold mountains of New England, and the Midwest, I am here to tell you that life is unpredictable. The moment I thought I had it figured out, here comes another challenge. Although I'm confident I have more to learn, here are a few lessons that left an indelible imprint on my spirit.

- If you make a mistake, admit it and don't lie. Other people know that you've made a mistake. The more you try to hide the lie, the worse it looks. My friend

William said it best: "Why lie when the truth will do?" I consider it extremely disrespectful when you lie to my face; this is what I expect of a child who's unaware of consequences. Let me share a secret: most people know you're lying.

- When I recruited prospective students, I briefly discussed one of our first-year seminars: Philosophy of Beauty. When asked, I found that a high number of young men considered themselves handsome. On the contrary, very few young women considered themselves beautiful. What are we teaching our young women about beauty? Our girls need constant reinforcement that they are beautiful beyond the physical. I admit that I lost my way a few times, but I always found my way back to the solid foundation of my upbringing. When someone loves you unconditionally, they will tell you you're beautiful, regardless of what someone else says. Stand confidently, and walk in a room like you own it. I never—and I mean never—thought about how I looked compared to other girls until I came to the United States. There was no conversation in my grandmother's house or my aunt's house about this topic. I thought how much someone loved you and how much they gave back to the community was what beauty was all about. Ugliness was bad behavior and mistreatment.

- Women, surround yourselves with a group of sisters who will have your back, front, and each side; they are my personal board of directors. I've had the same life mentor for thirty years. She hasn't steered me wrong; my front is covered. I have at least ten women whom I can call and cry; they will pray for me without explanation. My sisters speak my language, and they don't judge. My college familia (Lani, Ofie, Evonne, LT, Dee, C2) has my back. If I make one phone call or send a text, the Eastern Seaboard is meeting me in the Midwest. And my New York posse is lit. Right, V?

- Write your own narrative, or others will tell your story inaccurately and may attempt to smear your character. I told a supervisor that I refused to be disrespected by another woman who clearly had no self-confidence. It wasn't about the supervisor taking sides; my narrative mattered. A member of my board of directors told me years ago that there are three sides to a story: my side, your side, and the truth. No one else can tell your story like you can. It's an uphill battle, but it's absolutely possible to change the negative narrative.

- Trust me when I tell you that "perceived access to power" is a thing. If you report to, eat lunch with, sit next to, or according to Maya Angelou, "laugh like you've got gold mines diggin' in your backyard," folks really think you have power. I know perception isn't reality, but I've learned it's that person's reality. When I was promoted to assistant dean, there were people who believed I knew more information than I did because I reported directly to the dean. I had an agenda for each meeting, and after business concluded, unless we disagreed on the best hip-hop lyricist (Tupac or Biggie) or the amount of candy in his office, I wasn't privy to other information. Yet their imagination ran farther than Usain Bolt's best time in the 100-meter race. As I heard during an inclusion and equity workshop, people become emotionally hijacked when things don't work in their favor or when their actions obtain unintended results; they can't determine perception from reality. Access to power doesn't mean you have power, it means what it says: you have access, but that can mean a lot.

- Transformative leaders must know what's happening within their units; this is different from micromanagement. Whether it's the maintenance staff, the intern, the retired part-time employee or the volunteer, transformative leaders find the time to learn with and from them. I've heard that leaders just don't have the time to get into the weeds, and for this reason, middle management handles the mundane. What some leaders don't understand is that too often, people tell them what they want to hear, which may not necessarily be the truth. Effective, transformative leaders must make time with those who serve them daily. The TV show *Undercover Boss* is a great example of learning the truth; we need "truth" in higher education. Presidents, chancellors, provosts, deans, and vice presidents should consider taking the time to listen, reflect, communicate, and then act. Listening tours during the first few months are nice, but that's it, nice! However, if you're not going to be a transformative leader, why lead? Maybe it's time to go undercover to learn the real deal.

- Professional bullies exist, and it's so easy to give in to their demands out of fear of losing your job and livelihood. I. AM. NOT. AFRAID. Years ago, an administrator confronted me about a statement I made that she felt was unfavorable. What was unknown to the administrator is that I walked into this meeting, like all others, with an arsenal: the ancestors on my left, my grandmother on the right, God/Goddess in the front, and the voiceless sisters holding my back. I remained confident. During our conversation, I quickly realized that when you stand up for yourself and challenge someone in power, they're flabbergasted you would dare speak up and not back down. The administrator had supported me for years, but I questioned if the support was meant to keep me in the "sunken place." My point is: know the difference between critical feedback and professional bullying.

- My friend Dr. Bates had said time and again that one lesson she learned from her mother is that "your skin folk ain't always your kinfolk," and I couldn't agree more. Stop thinking that because people look like you, they will support you. Whether it's in the church, bedroom, boardroom, or neighborhood: Just Stop It.

- Learn when to say no and lean back. I realize it's popular to say yes and lean in. If that works for you, go forth and slay. However, always saying yes can't be done without self-sacrifice. Who will refuel and replenish your soul if you continue to say yes?

- You don't always have to be first; it's truly relative. That is just some psychological nonsense that people make us believe. Being first is impressive. It can give you credibility, but it's not the end of the world if you're not first. James Harrison, a linebacker for the Pittsburgh Steelers, was an undrafted free agent. Now he is one of the best players at his position. Antonio Brown was drafted in the sixth round out of seven in the NFL draft; he, too, is an excellent player, and he wasn't first. Yes, I'm a Steelers fan; I only roll with winners! For me, the real question is: what are you first in, and how are you helping others?

- You shouldn't keep company with others who are insecure and weren't raised to believe they were valued. That's all.

- Dream BIG (Bold, the Impossible, with Greatness)! I had goals and dreams, but I didn't always think boldly enough. I believed it was an exercise in futility, especially if I didn't have the resources to make them happen. I once thought, if the dream is impossible, why dream? Without dreams, you have no hope. As Langston Hughes said about a deferred dream: "Maybe it sags like a heavy load. Or does it explode?" I had explosive dreams. I was reminded by my sister Sonia that Muhammad Ali said that he was the greatest; imagine if we all thought as he did. We were born to be great; we must tap into that greatness. When my grandmother told me she loved me, I never questioned it. We wouldn't have to question how great we are if we really knew it. Whatever skills, tools, or credentials we need to get to greatness, GET IT. Time isn't guaranteed to anyone so what are you waiting for? Imagine what greatness Tupac, Trayvon Martin, Emmett Till, Sandra Bland, Tarika Wilson, Rekia Boyd, Sam DuBose, and countless others would've accomplished. Now is your time to demonstrate GREATNESS. My Dreamwalking Master Class with Sonia Jackson Myles completely transformed my dreams. I consider that experience my freedom blueprint. This book is a product of my revolutionary dream.

- I was a first-generation college student. Today, I encourage my family members to pursue a degree or any certificate that will help sustain the upward trajectory of the family. I pay my nieces for good grades, whatever it takes for them to get that degree. This is how I pay it forward.

- Your title, your degree, your position at work or at church are no indication that you're better or smarter than anyone else. Yes, you may have more funds in your bank account, access to people in higher positions, and possibly are able to afford workshops to enhance your skills. Ultimately, life's about making decisions that are right for you in that moment. When

124

my parents divorced, my mother literally left with nothing except her clothes and a few things she owned after twenty years. The "right" decision was to get a lawyer and request alimony and child support. Instead, she lived by the promise that God would provide. She received no alimony and only minimal child support, which was fifty dollars per week—for a ten-year-old—minus the fee charged at the check-cashing hotspot. She never mentioned it, but I'm certain there was some regret, as her life is drastically different now. But she didn't have time to crawl into a corner. Each day she woke up, dressed for work, put one foot in front of the other, and paid her bills. You must live with the decisions you make.

- I am not always the right messenger. I've learned if folks don't like the leader, they're not going to listen to or respect what that leader does or says. Years ago, as I led one of three formal meetings that I thought were essential, I realized that bodies were in the room, but I didn't garner their respect. They were not supportive of my role or position, and they made it known in their actions or lack thereof. Whether it was having a full conversation and snickering while I spoke or pretending they were clueless about events I spearheaded, I wasn't the right messenger for that group. The person who's liked, favored, or has given the most compliments will be more respected or heard. We must know when we're not the right messenger.

- Do not underestimate the power of common sense. We assume that people are knowledgeable because they have a college degree when, in reality, common sense was the only strategy needed. Over twenty years ago my mother said, "It doesn't matter where you get your degree, if you have no common sense, you're an educated fool." She was right.

- You will remember lessons from your parents, grandparents, guardian, teachers, mentors, or someone really important to you at a crucial point in your life. Be brave enough to call (not texting or using any form of social media) and tell that person that he or she was right. You will have that moment of clarity, and finally understand you were not the wisest person when you were younger.

- My aunt mentioned to me, "What happens at the shore is different than what happens in the ocean." At ten years old, I thought: what is she saying? Every time we go to the beach, she never gets in the water. She also talked to herself while washing clothes by hand and hanging them to dry on the clothesline in the sun. I really thought she was crazy. I once asked her, "Auntie, why do you talk to yourself?" She said, "No one can take my business anywhere or claim I said something I didn't." In my forties, I've lived a bit, and I can now relate.

- You must have a personal inventory of where people are in your life. I'm very deliberate about the people I select to spend time with, to have a meal with, and just relax with. I had a conversation with my friend Mandi about what happens when there's a violation of trust among friends. She may have compared it to being in a church choir. In the choir, people are in different rows and can be moved around from front, to middle, to the back of the choir depending on their behavior. My take was that *some* people deserved a second chance. However, I'm not moving folks around like they were in a choir. Some people just need to be put out of the church. After our discussion, I realized that maybe I needed to have a choir mentality. Maybe I was too harsh or drastic in cutting people off. The point is, it's essential to assess and evaluate what value the people in your life bring—whether or not they are worthy of your time and how you help each other with upward mobility. There's a middle ground between shifting rows and being completely out of the church. Find it. I have heard for many years that people are in your life for a reason, season, or a lifetime. We must understand when the reason or season is over, and we have to accept it.

- Other than unconditional love, there's nothing greater than feeling liberated. I was reminded by the body art of one of my former students that to be liberated is the freedom to think without distraction and the power to know when and how to stand up for yourself. Bob Marley reminded us in "Redemption Song," to "[e]mancipate yourselves from mental slavery; none but ourselves can free our minds." My freedom papers came a few years ago and unlike my naturalization papers, they cannot be revoked. I'm liberated to speak without being silenced and to walk into a room like Queen Nandi. I am liberated by the self-awareness that I am a Powerhouse!

Chapter Thirteen

Letter to My Daughter: Forgive Me

I know my mother helped raise you for ten long years while I pursued an education. I hope you didn't feel abandoned, but if you did, forgive me. You were always loved and my uttermost priority.

There were times when we didn't agree and my parenting style seemed too firm. Forgive me. I did what I thought was in your best interest as your mother.

Leaving New York City to live in New Hampshire wasn't ideal. No friends, no familiar faces, and the transition was far from perfect. Your dad and I made you as comfortable as possible in the new unwelcoming environment. Forgive me. We wanted to provide you with options other than the apartment in Harlem.

As a child, you thought you had two mothers: Ma and Mommy. At times you didn't know who should be your supporter or disciplinarian. Forgive me. I was the only person who made the decision to parent you alone; I didn't have another viable choice.

I didn't miss any birthdays, but I missed parent-teacher conferences, picking you up after school, and I attended limited school events. Forgive me. It wasn't intentional; I was preparing for the future.

You were taught to be an independent, adventurous, liberated young woman. You have more grit and gusto than I imagined. Forgive me. I didn't teach you to ask for help more often; life can become overwhelming.

I admire your smooth, chocolate complexion from head to toe. For this reason, I'm always kissing you on your silky, warm neck that always smells like lotion. This is the type of beauty that radiates without the sunlight. Forgive me. I wasn't explicit in our discussions that imbeciles will use your skin-tone to disparage you. As you've told me in my time of need, they are just haters. Your blackness and dark skin matter.

You have the talent and skills to set the world on fire with your unique gift for fashion design. Forgive me. I didn't teach you that the struggle is real. Hustling and who you know, at times, can take you further than a degree.

You deserve to be loved unconditionally, without question. I made sure you witnessed what affection, self-worth, and self-respect mean and look like. Forgive me. I didn't teach you that not all partners will be like your dad, and you'll have to do your own soul-searching, as I did, to find the one. Trust me, these relationships exist.

I love you. You are undoubtedly the wind beneath my wings. The sun rises with you in mind. The Caribbean Sea waves to you when you visit, and you give new meaning to the term "creative Goddess." Forgive me. I didn't tell you how much you are loved often enough.

Chapter Fourteen

#Black Lives Matter

I am angry, disturbed, outraged, and saddened by yet
again the murders of two other black men (Alton Sterling and
Philando Castile) by the hands of law enforcement. I know
when I'm stressed, it takes me longer to fall asleep, and my
thoughts are racing. My heart is beating faster than ever as I
watch black men moaning and gasping for air on TV for the
world to see. Did I see this before with Eric Garner? Did I
see the outrage, protests, marches, and vows for justice?
Tamir Rice's picture haunts me because I know his mother
didn't get justice. Can she sleep at night? How does she
handle his birthdays and holidays? I immediately thought of
my son who was visiting family in Virginia; I just wanted to
give him an extra hug. When my husband has business trips,
my last words are, "Get home safely." Every morning when I

drop off my son to school or he's leaving for the store, I tell him: "Get home safely." He doesn't know or understand the dangers of this world. However, I know it, you know it, and we all know that he's not immune from the violence. Yet I want to shield and protect him. After the death of Michael Brown three years ago, I told my son that I must demonstrate what he should do if he's stopped by the police. I gave him a set of instructions. In my kitchen, I told him to:

- Get on his knees.
- Place his hands behind the back of his head.
- DO NOT speak unless they ask you questions.
- DO NOT and I repeat DO NOT reach for your phone or your identification. Let them know both items are in your front pocket and you're too scared to reach for them.
- Yes sir, yes ma'am, and don't make eye contact.
- If you're arrested, ask to call your parents and invoke your rights as a citizen of this country.

134

Maybe I need to send him to a workshop to learn the proper procedures; I want him to live and get home safely. In the winter months, he loves his hoodie, and I tell him to take it off when he enters any building. However, he's a teenager, and I can't travel with him every moment of the day.

What else can I do to protect him? I had to take a step back, reflect, and ask myself if I was paranoid, overly sensitive, was it the recent news making me anxious, or was it racial trauma? My friend Tyree—a mother of four black young men—said she was having the same feelings of anxiety. Instead of talking about how to improve grades or become better students, their conversations shift to what her sons should do when stopped by the police. This is no way to live.

As black mothers, we pray, we cry, we hope, but what do we do when we've poured out our souls, the tears have dried,

135

and nothing has changed? It's painful and frustrating when there's no justice in sight. I have two years before he's off to college, and I'm going to hug him, love him, kiss him, and protect him as long as I can. I'm asking/begging my ancestors, Saint Bernadette, and my grandmother to watch over him. At times, I feel it's not enough.

My friends know I love the Incredible Hulk. He only emerged when pushed to the edge. I believe black mothers/parents have been pushed for so many years; unfortunately, society isn't ready to see the transformation. I will become the She-Hulk to protect my children and my black husband.

Chapter Fifteen

Being Bernadette

I grew up in my grandmother's four-bedroom, blue wooden house, and I always felt loved. There was a certain bond that couldn't be broken as the first grandchild. She taught me how to pray, become an entrepreneur, how to save money, cook and clean, the importance of kindness, and pray some more. She believed in tradition and although she was no longer a practicing Catholic, she thought it was important for me to go through the sacraments of the Catholic Church.

I was baptized at six weeks. At either seven or eight years old, I started classes for the confirmation process. I recall there were times I was confused as I knew we attended a different type of church (Church of God, Apostolic Faith), but I still had to go through the process. I was always inquisitive, but I knew not to ask why. Instead, I listened to the conversations of the elders. When I learned that I would be given a Catholic name, I thought my name would be too long; that meant I had two middle names. But who was Bernadette anyway? Yes, I knew she was a saint, but I didn't understand who she was until I became an adult. She was the young girl who had over a dozen visions and later became the saint of the sick and the poor. I thought it was a difficult name and responsibility to carry; after all, I was someone else.

I woke up at 6:30 or 7:00 a.m. during the week to get ready for school, and I was responsible for my sister Lisa. As the eldest child, I had to make sure both our uniforms were ironed—the pleats had to be just right; all students were checked for compliance with the uniform policy. We had breakfast: porridge cooked with milk (not water); or bread with butter and cheese, and ham roll; or fried eggs with sliced cucumbers and tomatoes on the side. Of course, we needed to have freshly brewed tea, picked directly from the plant in the yard. After we ate and got dressed, Lisa and I walked to school but had to make a quick stop to say good morning to auntie. She was my grandmother's eyes and ears, but she wasn't the only one.

Truthfully, the entire neighborhood saw everything; we wouldn't dare do or say anything we didn't want our grandmother to know. Most days, fear alone kept me on the straight and narrow. For some reason, Lisa didn't like school; it just wasn't her thing. I literally had to pull and drag her along so many mornings; she cried on her way to school but never on the way home.

I recently asked her what was the real issue. She mentioned school was boring, she hated the structure, the work was challenging, she sat for too long, and she was afraid of getting a beating if we were late. Most of her memories were being scared of school; she hated her experience. However, she loved recess.

On the island, students must be on their best behavior, corporal punishment was common for missed homework, disrespectful behavior, lateness, back talk, wrinkled uniforms, and a litany of what they deemed to be violation of school policy. I was definitely subject to corporal punishment twice to my memory and at least on one occasion for an incomplete assignment. I padded the back of my uniform with thin composition books to reduce the pain or laceration from the belt. I would've liked Saint Bernadette to make an appearance to save me, but she was nowhere to be found.

We lined up each morning in the schoolyard for uniform inspection, which included earrings and fingernail polish; I despised this show of power and control. It only takes one time to get a beating with the flat side of the ruler to learn that the right-size earrings (studs) were the only ones allowed. I'm not sure what the life lesson really was, but I just hope this ridiculous practice no longer exists.

After school, I stopped at the market to visit my grandmother who gave instructions for dinner preparation. If stew fish was the dinner of choice, my job was to scale, gut, season, fry, and then stew the fish. The process was easy enough, but the fish was cooked on a coal pot outside the house; we didn't want the entire house to smell like fish. Even when we opened all the windows, the smell of fish got into your clothes, furniture, and curtains. My grandmother made the rice, dumplings, or fungi (boiled corn meal, shaped in a small bowl) as the side dish with potato salad, sliced plantains, or boiled sweet potatoes. We all ate with a spoon (I still do). My grandfather ate with a fork, spoon, and a knife; he used the spoon mainly when he had gravy or anything that couldn't really fit on the fork. I believe that was more of the formal, British dining etiquette. Dishes were washed by hand and the table cleaned before I even considered playing outside with friends; and we had to ask permission to go out. My grandmother wanted to know who, where, how long, and if we left out any information, we had to check-in. We were under my grandmother's watchful eyes. She always said, "You muda lef you wid me and me go mek sure she get de two all you ina one piece."

We had one black and white TV in the house, which meant we watched whatever my grandparents wanted. *The Beverly Hillbillies, Gunsmoke, Mousercise, The Jeffersons, Sanford and*

Son, everything religious, the local news, BBC, and like clockwork, wrestling. My grandmother talked to the characters as if she was in the audience and dozed off several times, but we wouldn't dare change the channel. When we begged her to change the channel after the cup, bowl, hand towel, or whatever item she had in her hands fell to the floor, she claimed she only closed her eyes for one minute. As an adult, I can laugh at this memory, but at the time, I didn't understand it—but should I? She worked all day, sun up to sundown; she deserved to have the TV on any channel if she wanted, with no interruptions.

My grandmother was the first entrepreneur in the house. A few days during the week, with the perishable items that were not sold at the market, I walked the neighborhood selling them to make extra money. We sold mangoes, green and ripe bananas, sweet potatoes, green vegetables, roasted peanuts, and anything else grown on a small farm or bought from the Dominicans (not Dominican Republic) at the wharf.

What Americans call desserts were made with love and special ingredients only a few in the family knew. I was always the taste tester for the bread-and-potato pudding with raisins, coconut tarts, and homemade ginger beer. She taught me how to make ginger beer, and I am best in the family.

I only took the ripe bananas and mangoes around the neighborhood, and with a wooden tray on my head, using a hand-rolled thick cloth as a barrier between the tray and my head, I yelled, "Geeeetttt yo mangoes, geeeetttt yo ripe figs." We rarely called them bananas: they were ripe figs. Most days, I sold almost all items; I was really good.

The patrons at the market called me a "hustler" because I knew how to weigh the products with my hands, without putting the produce on the scale. Of course, they thought I was cheating, but eight out of ten times, I was right. Some people who knew my other grandmother (father's mother), thought I had her alleged obeah (witchcraft) skills. I didn't know if that was meant as a compliment; I doubt it. Maybe Saint Bernadette blessed my hands and was the driving force behind the scale.

My entrepreneurial skills came in handy when I competed in the school's pageant show; my talent was an ethnic dance along with satire about selling goods in the neighborhood. I was so excited when I was announced second runner-up, one step away from representing the school at the island's annual Miss Antigua Teen Pageant. It was a proud moment for my family.

If we were sick, the doctor's office was not the first stop; we had homemade concoctions. There were times I had a high fever; I was literally burning up. Before 6:00 p.m., my grandmother knew she had to pick soursop and guava leaves from the yard—don't ask why she had to pick them before 6:00 p.m., maybe it was cultural. First, she would give me a warm bath with different types of leaves; the concoction didn't smell good together. I had to sit and soak in the large, galvanized steel tub we had. She would massage my back with the leaves similar to patting a baby's back after eating for a burp. As a preteen, I couldn't complain that I was too grown for this remedy. I couldn't dry off; the concoction had to soak through my skin. I put on my nightgown and got into bed under the covers. I drank hot tea, she rubbed my skin with the green rubbing alcohol, stuffed the soursop leaves down my nightgown, and then tied a belt or string around my waist so that the leaves didn't fall out. A bandana was soaked with the rubbing alcohol and tied around my head with half of a green lime, pulp side on my forehead. She prayed, read passages from the Bible, made the sign of the cross, and told me stories of her childhood until I fell asleep.

Within twenty-four hours, my fever was reduced, and when we removed the belt or string from my waist, the leaves fell to the floor, and they were completely dry. It was easy to hear them fall on the wooden floor, and we knew I would be ready for school the next day. I always thought the remedy was amazingly miraculous, and it worked every time. However, I wondered if Saint Bernadette played a role; she was directly connected to God. If the fever didn't break within two days, only then was a doctor considered for modern medicine.

At least three days per week, church was a major part of my life. First, Sunday school, then church service until the Spirit moved the congregation to end. Of course, we had to return for the evening service at 7:00. One of the brothers or the ministers from the church usually gave us a ride home, but occasionally, we walked. It really wasn't a long walk, but as a child when I fell asleep in church, walking was the last thing I wanted to do.

One of my pet peeves was certainly the ten percent my grandmother always placed in the collection plate. I knew she didn't have the money, but she felt compelled or pressured, moved by the love of God or notice of the minister, or needed some assurance that she would get to heaven by paying her tithes. Don't get me wrong, I believe in giving to the place of worship, but there's so much pressure to give when you don't have enough for the food on your table. Fortunately, food insecurity wasn't our story, but it was the story of many. Keep in mind, there was money in the collection plate Sunday morning and when we returned that evening—and God forbid we had the "special offering" for the pastor, more money. When we had prayer meetings, there was the collection plate, and if there was a program during the week, the collection plate made another round. As a child, I just thought it was too much.

I learned about money early in life as my grandmother always demonstrated the skills of saving as much as possible and finding good places to hide the money. She may have had a bank account, but I knew that the real savings was under the mattress, at the bottom on the left, folded in a plastic bag, in a certain location. She kept the total amount separate, so whether anyone tried to take a dollar or five dollars, she knew the account balance. My grandmother was the smartest, most humorous woman I knew; she was my first prayer warrior.

Epilogue

Black Girl Magic

I've had to dig deeper, dream bigger, and climb higher as a black, immigrant woman living in America. I had to be honest about who I am. I have acknowledged that I despise the rules if they're not fair and just. Black girl magic is demanding systemic changes, even if I am the only one standing.

My black girl magic is the resilience needed to stare down microaggressive behaviors and intimidation, which show up in forms of smiles, niceties, and well-intended commentary. This type of resilience isn't for the faint of heart; my sisters have stepped up beside me and held the torch of freedom.

My black girl magic is coloring outside the lines and loving the new art with no apologies and having the confidence to know it's worth more than I am being paid.

My black girl magic is knowing that there's nothing polite about silence when racial violence rears its ugly head. Nonetheless, I can rise like a phoenix and use the fire within me to clear the path for others.

My black girl magic is stepping out of my comfort zone with the courage to fail, make mistakes, and convince others failure isn't the end; it revealed my true self. I've had to conjure Saint Bernadette with the realization that she can't save me from professional bullies, wannabe cartoonists, and racial trauma. My black girl magic is accepting that my education from a top liberal arts college doesn't make me immune from the harsh reality that naturalization papers and citizenship aren't the only requirements for the American dream. It's a personal journey that needs tremendous grit. I didn't imagine that the young girl from an unrecognizable island on the world map, known for its 365 beaches, would become anything more than the average girl from the South Bronx who wanted to live a normal Antiguan-American life. I should've listened to my grandmother who told me I was special, loved, and blessed beyond imagination. Today, I know she was referring to the black girl magic that would emerge when I needed it most. I continue to use my voice and black girl magic to shed light on the marginalized, motivate others to speak their truth, and empower other women to unleash their black girl magic.

For You, Grandma

Psalm 27

The Lord is my light and my salvation—
    whom shall I fear?
The Lord is the stronghold of my life—
    of whom shall I be afraid?
When evil men advance against me
    To devour my flesh,
when my enemies and my foes attack me,
    they will stumble and fall.
Though an army besiege me,
    my heart will not fear;
though war break out against me,
    even then will I be confident.

One thing I ask from the lord,
    this is what I seek:
that I may dwell in the house of the Lord
    all the days of my life,
        to gaze upon the beauty of the Lord
        and to seek him in his temple.
For in the day of trouble
    he will keep me safe in his dwelling;
he will hide me in the shelter of his tabernacle
    and set me high upon a rock.
Then my head will be exalted
    above the enemies who surround me;
    at his tabernacle will I sacrifice with

shouts of joy,
I will sing and make music to the Lord.

Hear my voice when I call, O Lord;
    be merciful to me and answer me.
My heart says of you, "Seek his face!"
    Your face, Lord, I will seek.
Do not hide your face from me,
    do not turn your servant away in anger,
    you have been my helper.

Do not reject me or forsake me,
    O God my Savior.
Though my father and mother forsake me,
    the Lord will receive me.
Teach me your way, O Lord;
    lead me in a straight path
    because of my oppressors.
Do not turn me over to the desire of my foes,
    for false witnesses rise up against me,
    breathing out violence.

I am still confident of this:
    I will see the goodness of the Lord
    in the land of the living.
Wait for the Lord;
    be strong and take heart
    and wait for the Lord.

Afterword

"I don't have to be what you want me to be. I am free to be what I want."—attributed to Muhammad Ali

Writing this memoir has been the most challenging project I've worked on for at least a decade. It has been cathartic and liberating and undoubtedly an integral part of my healing process. As I skimmed through my journal entries for the past four years, I realized that in December 2013, I wrote that my story will become a memoir. Be careful what you write and give energy; you will only need a nudge to make it a reality.

There were times I questioned whether I should make myself vulnerable, but the freedom to speak and to be heard overshadowed any doubts I had. We must all live our truth. When I couldn't find the words, my life mentor, Ms. Murphy, reminded me that I should speak from the heart and I did.

I continue to repeat my self-affirmation created

during my Dreamwalking Masterclass:

I love myself because I am confident.
I will not be distracted by how others perceive me;
I will change the narrative.
What matters is that I am a good mother,
caring daughter, patient sister, and loving wife.

My next project is on the horizon. I will share my ten

commandments for women who serve in higher education.

It's time to dismantle and disrupt the systemic injustices that

keep women from reaching their highest potential.

REFERENCES

Chapter 10: The Darker the Flesh, the Deeper the Roots

Angelou, Maya. 1978. "Still I Rise." *And Still I Rise: A Book of Poems.* New York: Random House.

Dunbar, Paul Laurence. 1896. "We Wear the Mask." *Lyrics of Lowly Life.* Shmoop University, Inc. Last modified November 11, 2008. Accessed October 14, 2017. https://www.shmoop.com/we-wear-the-mask/.

X, Malcolm. 1962. Who Taught You to Hate Yourself? Annotated text of speech given at the funeral service of Ronald Stokes, Los Angeles. [online] Genius. Accessed October 24, 2017. https://genius.com/Malcolm-x-who-taught-you-to-hate-yourself-annotated.

For You, Grandma: Psalm 27

Holy Bible. Ps. 27:1–14. 1973, 1978, 1984, 2011. New International Version. Biblica, Inc.

About the Author

Carol Tonge Mack is an educator, black feminist, and student advocate. She has been working for the past twenty years in higher education and began her professional career as an academic advisor at the University of New Hampshire. Carol believes in the power of "real" sisterhood and helping women recognize they are good enough, regardless if they are holding a broom or the gavel. Currently, she is an assistant dean at the University of Cincinnati, serving and empowering students from enrollment to graduation.

Carol received her bachelor's degree in history from Middlebury College in Vermont, her master of arts in teaching, as well as a master of education in counseling from the University of New Hampshire. A native of the Caribbean island of Antigua, Carol grew up in the South Bronx, New York City; her extended family resides in Harlem, New York. She has two amazing children and is also married to an organic chemistry professor.

Made in the USA
Lexington, KY
17 January 2018